SURRENDERING TO JESUS

6 SMALL GROUP SESSIONS ON WORSHIP

STUDENT EDITION

DOUG FIELDS & BRETT EASTMAN

ZONDERVAN™

GRAND RAPIDS, MICHIGAN 49530 USA

ZONDERVAN.COM/
AUTHORTRACKER

Youth Specialties

www.youthspecialties.com

Surrendering to Jesus, Student Edition: Six Sessions on Worship
Copyright © 2006 by Doug Fields and Brett Eastman

Youth Specialties products, 300 South Pierce Street, El Cajon, CA 92020,
are published by Zondervan, 5300 Patterson Avenue SE, Grand Rapids,
MI 49530

Library of Congress Cataloging-in-Publication Data

Fields, Doug, 1962-
  Surrendering to Jesus : 6 small group sessions on worship / Doug Fields
and Brett Eastman.
    p. cm. -- (Experiencing Christ together, student edition)
  ISBN-10: 0-310-26649-1 (pbk.)
  ISBN-13: 978-0-310-26649-5 (pbk.)
  1. Worship--Biblical teaching. 2. Worship--Study and teaching. I.
Eastman, Brett, 1959- II. Title.
BV10.3.F54 2006
268'.433--dc22

                                                    2005024177

---

*Creative Team: Dave Urbanski, Holly Sharp, Mark Novelli, Joanne Heim,
Janie Wilkerson*
Cover Design: Mattson Creative
Printed in the United States of America

---

08 09 10 • 10 9 8 7 6 5 4

ACKNOWLEDGMENTS

This series of six books couldn't have happened if there weren't some wonderful friends who chimed in on the process and added their heart and level of expertise to these pages. I need to acknowledge and thank my friends for loving God, caring for students and supporting me-especially true on this task were Amanda Maguire, Nancy Varner, Ryanne Dearden, Jana Sarti, Matt McGill and the crew at Simply Youth Ministry. I sure appreciate doing life together. Also, I'm very appreciative of Brett Eastman for asking me to do this project.

TABLE OF CONTENTS

INTRODUCTION: READ ME FIRST!

Welcome to a Journey with Jesus (and Others)!

I hope you're ready for God to do something great in your life as you use this book and connect with a few friends and a loving small group leader. The potential of this combination is incredible. The reason we know its potential is because we've heard from thousands of students who've already gone through our first series of LIFETOGETHER books and shared their stories. We've been blessed to hear that the combination of friends gathering together, books with great questions, and the Bible as a foundation have provided the ingredients for life change. As you read these words, know that you're beginning a journey that may revolutionize your life.

The following six sessions are designed to help you grow in your knowledge of Jesus and his teachings and become his devoted disciple. But growth doesn't happen alone. You need God's help and a community of people who love God, too. We've found that a great way to grow strong in Christ is in the context of a caring, spiritual community (or small group). This community is committed to doing life together—at least for a season—and will thrive when each small group member (you) focuses on Jesus as well as the others in the group.

This type of spiritual community isn't easy. It requires several things from you:

- trust
- confidentiality
- honesty
- care
- openness
- risk
- commitment to meet regularly

Anyone can meet with a few people and call it a "group," but it takes stronger commitment and desire to create a spiritual community where others can know you, love you, care for you, and give you the freedom to open up about your thoughts, doubts, and struggles—a place where you're safe to be yourself.

We've learned from the small groups that didn't work that spiritual community can't develop without honesty. Now, at first you may be tempted to show up to your small group session and sit, smile, act nicely, and never speak from your heart—but this type of superficial participation prevents true spiritual community. Please fight through this temptation and know that when you reveal who you really are, you'll contribute something unique and powerful to the group that can't occur any other way. Your honest sharing about your heart and soul will challenge other group members to do the same, and they'll likely become as honest as you are.

To help you get to this place of honesty, every session contains questions that are intended to push you to think, talk, and open your heart. They'll challenge you to expose some of your fears, hurts, and habits. Through them, I guarantee you'll experience spiritual growth and relational intimacy, and you'll build lasting, genuine friendships.

All mature Christians will tell you that God used others to impact their lives. God has a way of allowing one life to connect with another to result in richer, deeper, and more vibrant lives for both. As you go through this book (and the five others in this series), you will have the opportunity to impact someone else—and someone else will have the opportunity to impact you. You'll both become deeper, stronger followers of Jesus Christ. So get ready for some life change.

WHO IS JESUS?

Most people have an opinion about Jesus. But many of these opinions are based on what they've heard or come up with on their own—what they'd *prefer* Jesus to be—as opposed to their own discovery of Jesus through the Bible. People believe Jesus was all kinds of things—a great teacher, a leader of a revolution, a radical with a political agenda, a gentle man with a big vision, a prophet, a spiritual person who emphasized religion. Still others believe he is who he claimed to be—God.

The Jesus of the Bible is far more compelling than most people's opinions about him. *Surrendering to Jesus* allows you to get to know Jesus as his first followers did. They met Jesus as Teacher, a rabbi. They came to know Jesus as Healer, Shepherd, Servant, Savior, and ultimately the One who defeated death—the risen Lord. From his first words, "Follow me," through his ministry, death, and resurrection, he kept drawing people deeper into his life.

Jesus asked his disciples to commit their lives to God's way. As you read the Bible, you'll see that God's ways weren't always easy or comfortable for the disciples to follow. But what motivated them to do what he taught was their rich experience of who he was and all he did for them. *Surrendering to Jesus* will ground you in that same experience so you'll more fully desire to follow Jesus and commit to his ways—even when it's not easy or comfortable. The Jesus you're about to encounter is waiting for you to meet him, get closer to him, and commit your life to following his ways and teachings.

When you align your life with Jesus, you're in for a wild, adventurous life. It won't be without its difficulties, but it'll be a better life than you ever dreamed possible.

WHAT YOU NEED TO KNOW ABOUT EACH OF THESE SIX SESSIONS

Each session in this study contains more material than you and your group can complete in a typical meeting of an hour or so. The key to making the most of each session is to choose which questions you'll answer and discuss and which ones you'll save for your alone time. We've tried to make it simple, so if you miss something from one meeting, you can pick it up the next time you're together. Let's be more specific.

Each of the six sessions in *Surrendering to Jesus* contains five unique sections. These five sections have the same titles in every book and in every session in the LIFETOGETHER series. The sections are (1) fellowship, (2) discipleship, (3) ministry, (4) evangelism, and (5) worship. These represent five biblical purposes that we believe lead to personal spiritual growth, growth in your student ministry, and health for your entire church. The more you think about these five purposes and try to make them part of your life, the stronger you'll be and the more you'll grow spiritually.

While these five biblical purposes make sense individually, they can make a greater impact when they're brought together. Think of it in sports terms: If you play baseball or softball, you might be an outstanding hitter—but you also need to catch, throw, run, and slide. You need more than one skill to impact your team. In the same way, having a handle on one or two of the five biblical purposes is great—but when they're all reflected together in a person's life, that person is much more biblically balanced and healthy.

You'll find that the material in this book (and in the other LIFETOGETHER books) is built around the Bible. There are a lot of blank spaces and journaling pages where you can write down your thoughts about God's Word and God's work in your life as you explore and live out God's biblical purposes.

Each session begins with a short story that helps introduce the theme. If you have time to read it, great—if not, no big deal. Immediately following the story are five key sections. The following is a brief description of each:

♥ FELLOWSHIP: CONNECTING YOUR HEART TO OTHERS

Goal: To share about your life and listen attentively to others, caring about what they share

You'll begin your session with a few minutes of conversation that will give you all a chance to share from your own lives, get to know each other better, and offer initial thoughts about the session's theme. The icon for this section is a heart because you're opening up your heart so others can connect with you on a deeper level.

DISCIPLESHIP: GROWING TO BE LIKE JESUS

Goal: To explore God's Word, gain biblical knowledge, and make personal applications

This section will take the most time. You'll explore the Bible and gain some knowledge about Jesus. You'll encounter his life and teachings and discuss how God's Word can make a difference in your own life. The icon for this section is a brain because you're opening your mind to learn God's Word and his ways.

You'll find lots of questions in this section—more than you can discuss during your group time. Your leader will choose the questions you have time to discuss or come up with different questions. We encourage you to respond to the skipped questions on your own; during the week it's a great way to get more Bible study time.

MINISTRY: SERVING OTHERS IN LOVE

Goal: To recognize and take advantage of opportunities to serve others

When you get to this section, you'll have an opportunity to discuss how to express God's love through serving others. The discussion and opportunities are created to tie into the topic. As you grow spiritually, you'll naturally begin to recognize and take opportunities to serve others. As your heart grows, so will your opportunities to serve. Here, the icon is a foot because feet communicate movement and action—serving and meeting the needs of others requires you to act on what you've learned.

EVANGELISM: SHARING YOUR STORY AND GOD'S STORY

Goal: To consider how the truths from this session might be applied to your relationships with unbelievers

It's very easy for a small group to turn into a clique that only looks inward and loses sight of others outside the group. That's not God's plan. God wants you to reach out to people with his message of love and life change. While this is often scary, this section will give you an opportunity to discuss your relationships with non-Christians and consider ways to listen to their stories, share pieces of your story, and reflect the amazing love of God's story. The icon for this section is a mouth because you're opening your mouth to have spiritual conversations with nonbelievers.

WORSHIP: SURRENDERING YOUR LIFE TO HONOR GOD

Goal: To focus on God's presence

Each session ends with a time of prayer. You'll be challenged to slow down and turn your focus toward God's love, his goodness, and his presence in your life. You'll spend time talking to God, listening in silence, reading Scripture, writing, and focusing on God. The key word for this time is *surrender*, which is giving up what you want so God can give you what he wants. The icon for this section is a body, which represents surrendering your entire life to God.

Oh yeah…there are more sections in each session!

In addition to the main material, there are several additional options you can use to help further and deepen your times with God. Many people attend church programs, listen, and then "leave" God until the next week when they return to church. We don't want that to happen to you! So we've provided several more opportunities for you to learn, reflect, and grow on your own.

At the end of every session you'll find three more key headings:

- At Home This Week
- Learn a Little More
- For Deeper Study on Your Own

They're fairly easy to figure out, but here's a brief description of each:

AT HOME THIS WEEK

There are five options presented at the end of each session that you can do on your own. They're not homework for the next session (unless your leader assigns them to your group); they're things you can do to keep growing at your own pace. You can skip them, you can do all of them, or you can vary the options from session to session.

Option 1: A Weekly Reflection

At the end of each session you'll find a one-page, quick self-evaluation that helps you reflect on the five key areas of your spiritual life (fellowship, discipleship, ministry, evangelism, and worship). It's simply a guide for you to gauge your spiritual health. The first one begins on page 28.

Option 2: Daily Bible Readings

One of the challenges in deepening your knowledge of God's Word and learning more about Jesus' life is to read the Bible on your own. This option provides a guide to help you read through the Psalms in 30 days. On pages 113-114 is a list of Bible passages to help you continue to take God's Word deeper into your life.

Option 3: Memory Verses

On pages 118-119 you'll find six Bible verses to memorize. Each is related to the theme of a particular session. (Again, these are optional...remember, nothing is mandatory!)

Option 4: Journaling

You'll find a question or two related to the theme of the session that can serve as a trigger to get you writing. Journaling is a great way to reflect on what you've been learning and evaluate your life. In addition to questions at the end of each session, there's a helpful tool on pages 120-122 that can guide you through the discipline of journaling.

Option 5: Wrap It Up

As you've already read, each session contains too many questions for one small group meeting. So this section provides opportunities to think through your answers to the questions you skipped and then go back and write them down.

LEARN A LITTLE MORE

We've provided some insights (or commentary) on some of the passages that you'll study to help you understand the difficult terms, phrases, and people that you'll read about in each Bible passage.

FOR DEEPER STUDY ON YOUR OWN

One of the best ways to understand the Bible passages and the theme of each session is to dig a little deeper. If deeper study fits your personality style, please use these additional ideas as ways to enhance your learning.

WHAT YOU NEED TO KNOW ABOUT BEING IN A SMALL GROUP

You probably have enough casual or superficial friendships and don't need to waste your time cultivating more. We all need deep and committed friendships. Here are a few ideas to help you benefit the most from your small group time and build great relationships.

Prepare to Participate

Interaction is a key to a good small group. Talking too little will make it hard for others to get to know you. Everyone has something to contribute—yes, even you! But participating doesn't mean dominating, so be careful to not monopolize the conversation. Most groups typically have one conversation hog, and if you don't know who it is in your small group, then it might be you. Here's a tip: You don't have to answer every question and comment on every point. Try to find a balance between the two extremes.

Be Consistent

Healthy relationships take time to grow. Quality time is great, but a great quantity of time is probably better. Commit with your group to show up every week (or whenever your group plans to meet), even when you don't feel like it. With only six sessions per book, if you miss just two meetings you'll have missed a third of what's presented in these pages. When you make a commitment to your small group a high priority, you're sure to build meaningful relationships.

Practice Honesty and Confidentiality

Strong relationships are only as solid as the trust they are built upon. Although it may be difficult, take a risk and be honest with your answers. God wants you to be known by others! Then respect the risks others are taking and offer them the same love, grace, and forgiveness God does. Make confidentiality a nonnegotiable value for your small group. Nothing kills community like gossip.

Arrive Ready to Grow

You can always arrive prepared by praying ahead of time. Ask God to give you the courage to be honest and the discipline to respect others.

You aren't required to do any preparation in the book before you arrive (unless you're the leader—see page 82). If your leader chooses to, she may ask you to do the Discipleship

Doug Fields & Brett Eastman

Doug and Brett were part of the same small group for several years. Brett was the pastor of small groups at Saddleback Church where Doug is the pastor to students. Brett and a team of friends wrote DOING LIFETOGETHER, a group study for adults. Everyone loved it so much that they asked Doug to take the same theme and Bible verses and revise the other material for students. So even though Brett and Doug both had a hand in writing this book, the book you're using is written by Doug—and as a youth pastor, he's cheering you on in your small group experience. For more information on Doug and Brett see page 143.

section ahead of time so that you'll have more time to discuss the other sections and make better use of your time.

Congratulations...

...for making a commitment to go through this material with your small group! Life change is within reach when people are united through the same commitment. Your participation in a small group can have a lasting and powerful impact on your life. Our prayer is that the questions and activities in this book help you grow closer to the other group members, and more importantly, to God.

If you're a small group leader, please turn to page 83 for a brief instruction on how best to use this material.

SMALL GROUP COVENANT

One of the signs of a healthy small group is that all members understand its purpose. We've learned that members of good small groups make a bond, a commitment, or a covenant to one another.

Read through the following covenant as a group. Be sure to discuss your concerns and questions before you begin your first session. Please feel free to modify the covenant based on the needs and concerns of your particular group. Once you agree with the terms and are willing to commit to the covenant (as you've revised it), sign your own book and have the others sign yours.

With a covenant, your entire group will have the same purpose for your time together, allowing you to grow together and go deeper into your study of God's Word. Without a covenant, groups often find themselves meeting simply for the sake of meeting.

If your group decides to add some additional values, write them at the bottom of the covenant page. Your group may also want to create some rules (such as not interrupting when someone else is speaking or sitting up instead of lying down). You can list those at the bottom of the covenant page also.

Reviewing your group's covenant, values, and rules before each meeting can become a significant part of your small group experience.

A covenant is a binding agreement or contract. God made covenants with Noah, Abraham, and David, among others. Jesus is the fulfillment of a new covenant between God and his people.

SMALL GROUP COVENANT

I, _____, as a member of our small group, acknowledge my need for meaningful relationships with other believers. I agree that this small group community exists to help me deepen my relationships with God, Christians, and other people in my life. I commit to the following:

Consistency
I will give my best effort to attend each of our group meetings.

Honesty
I will take risks to share truthfully about the personal issues in my life.

Confidentiality
I will support the foundation of trust in our small group by not participating in gossip. I will not reveal personal information shared by others during our meetings.

Respect
I will help create a safe environment for our small group members by listening carefully and not making fun of others.

Prayer
I commit to pray regularly for the people in our small group.

Accountability
I will allow the people in my small group to hold me accountable for growing spiritually and living a life that honors God.

This covenant, signed by all the members in this group, reflects our commitment to one another.

Date:

Names:

Additional values our small group members agree to

Additional rules our small group members agree to

SESSION 1
FAITH THROUGH A STORM

 LEADERS, READ PAGE 82.

Andy's parents were getting a divorce. He knew they loved him, and he knew his parents were having a rough time, but Andy didn't understand such a drastic decision. It created so many questions and confusion about God's plan for his life. Andy couldn't imagine that this was what God wanted for his family. He started to doubt God's faithfulness and lose trust in the promises he'd learned as a young Christian. Andy feared he would lose the life he'd always known—and always wanted. It was hard for him to believe that God could work in this situation.

Andy asked his small group to pray, and the group dedicated an entire meeting to pray with Andy and talk about his family's circumstances. They discussed the reality of "storms" that come into our lives and talked about what it means to trust God in difficult times. Andy's small group committed to pray with Andy and ask about his family's situation each week. They stayed by his side during the entire divorce process.

Through this storm, Andy began to see that God was using his small group to keep him afloat. It didn't happen overnight, but eventually Andy surrendered his fears and uncertainties to God. When he finally let God deal with his pain, he felt secure that God would care for and love him and his family. Andy learned that when you surrender your life to God, you're able to see God in the midst of the storms—and you realize that he was there the entire time. In this session we'll learn about faith in difficult times.

♥ FELLOWSHIP: CONNECTING YOUR HEART TO OTHERS

Goal: To share about your life and listen attentively to others, caring about what they share

If you're new to this series of books, you'll find that every time you get to the fellowship section, the questions are designed to get you talking and knowing each other better. If you're a veteran of the series (which means that you've been through some of the other books), then you already know what to do.

A surrendered life begins with trust—trusting that God is who he says he is even in the midst of life's storms. Different people respond to life's storms in different ways. When you're in a small group, it's helpful to know how each person responds to storms or troubles so you can know how best to help each other.

Just a reminder: There probably isn't enough time in your small-group session to answer every question. Instead choose which ones you'll answer, and then answer the others on your own time. Have fun!

1. How do you typically respond when trouble hits your life? (Select all that apply.)

   - I panic.
   - I worry.
   - I become emotional.
   - I try to fix everything.
   - I handle a quick storm well, but if the painful situation goes on and on, it's really hard for me.
   - I become hyperactive.

- I try to distract myself with food, entertainment, the Internet, work, shopping, or_____

  _____.
- I talk to friends.
- I withdraw.
- I get depressed.
- I pray...eventually.
- I pray right away.
- I ask people for help.
- Other:

2. Have you ever had a near-death experience? If so, describe it.

If your group hasn't discussed the small group covenant on page 18, please take some time now to go through it. Make commitments to each other that your group time will reflect those values (and any additional ones you add). One sign of a healthy small group is that it begins each session by reading the covenant together as a constant reminder of what the group has committed to.

DISCIPLESHIP: GROWING TO BE LIKE JESUS

Goal: To explore God's Word, gain biblical knowledge, and make personal applications

Throughout history God has pursued us. He wants us to belong to his family, experience his presence, and fulfill his plans for our lives. God has done everything to make a relationship with him possible. God is the one who created us, loves us, and makes forgiveness available.

A central Christian belief is that Jesus died on the cross as payment for our sins. Faith (in Jesus' death and resurrection—which we'll discuss in session 6) is essential for our relationship with God. Many hazards, storms, and distractions will challenge our faith, but God is always faithful in our time of need. For example, just when the disciples thought Jesus was asleep during their troubles, he showed up in a big way.

Read Mark 4:35-41. (If you don't have a Bible, the passage is on page 87.)

1. Describe the scene by answering the following questions:

   Who was there?

   What time of day did this take place?

   What did the disciples do when the waves started to break over the boat?

   Why did they respond that way?

2. Why do you think the disciples questioned Jesus' compassion for them?

3. Are you facing any storms in your life right now? If so, how are you relying on Jesus?

4. In your opinion, how is fear an enemy of faith?

5. Why were the disciples still terrified after Jesus calmed the storm (verse 41)?

6. Describe what you think a faith-filled response from the disciples would have looked like in the midst of the storm.

7. What happens to you when your faith is hassled by fear or distraction? How does this affect your relationships with other people? With God?

8. Is there anything in your life right now that's distracting you from your faith? If so, what is it?

9. How has God helped you in the past with storms you've faced?

For the health of your small group, be sure to read the clique section on pages 102-103. It's vital for your group to decide at this first session whether you can invite friends to join your group. Talk about the structure of your group and stick to your decision. If you decide the answer is no, you may be able to invite friends to join you in the next EXPERIENC-ING CHRIST TO-GETHER book—there are six of them, so there's plenty of time! If you're a small-group leader, see the Small Group Leader Check-list on page 82.

MINISTRY: **SERVING** OTHERS IN LOVE

Goal: To recognize and take advantage of opportunities to serve others

Storms are everywhere. You can't always predict them; you don't always see them coming; and they hit some people harder than others. The reality is that storms just happen. If you haven't faced a storm that's threatened your spiritual health, be prepared for its arrival sometime down the line.

1. How can you help others who are experiencing storms?

2. What are some common mistakes people make when they're trying to "help" others?

3. How would your answer differ if the person in the storm did not have faith in Jesus?

EVANGELISM: **SHARING** YOUR STORY AND GOD'S STORY

Goal: To consider how the truths from this session might be applied to your relationships with unbelievers

1. How can your life serve as a testimony to others by the way you handle storms?

2. What do you think non-Christians see when they look at Christians who are experiencing storms?

3. Do you think God can use storms as a way to evangelize? Explain your answer.

🚶 WORSHIP: SURRENDERING YOUR LIFE TO HONOR GOD

Goal: To focus on God's presence

If you make it a habit to worship God during your times with him, your trust in God will grow because worship helps you focus on what makes God trustworthy. Worship strengthens us for the tough times.

1. How would you describe the current condition of your spiritual life? Are you growing? Coasting? Do you have doubts about something specific? Share your answer with the group.

2. Take a little time by yourself and set a goal to increase your practice of worship while you're going through this book. Your ideas might include a commitment to attend a worship service, 10 minutes a day of private worship, listening to a worship CD, committing to tithe your income, journaling about why you're thankful, reading God's Word, or something else along these lines. (All of the psalms are excellent for worship; a few to start with are Psalm 89, 92, 95-98, 103-104, 111, 136, 138, and 145-150.)

3. Read Psalm 31 aloud as a group. (If you don't have a Bible, the passage is on pages 87-90.) When you finish, add your own words of praise.

4. Close your time together in prayer.

You'll find three prayer resources in the appendices in the back of this book. By reading them (and possibly discussing them), you'll find your group prayer time more rewarding.
• Praying in Your Small Group (pages 129-130). Read this article on your own before the next session.
• Prayer Request Guidelines (pages 131-132). Read and discuss these guidelines as a group.
• Prayer Options (pages 133-134). Refer to this list for ideas to add variety to your prayer time.

AT HOME THIS WEEK

One of the consistent values of our LIFETOGETHER books is that we want you to have options for growing spiritually on your own during the week. To help with this "on your own" value, we'll give you five options. If you do these, you'll have more to contribute when you return to your small group, and you'll begin to develop spiritual habits that can last your entire life. Here are the five you'll see after every section. (You might try to do one per day on the days after your small group meets.)

Option 1: A Weekly Reflection

After each session you'll find a quick, one-page self-evaluation that reflects the five areas of your spiritual life found in this book (fellowship, discipleship, ministry, evangelism, and worship). After each evaluation, you decide if there's anything you'll do differently with your life. This page is all for you. It's not intended as a report card that you turn into your small group leader. The first evaluation is on pages 29-30.

Option 2: Daily Bible Readings

On pages 113-114 you'll find a list of Bible passages that will help you read through an entire section of the Bible in 30 days. If you choose this option, try to read one of the assigned passages each day. Highlight key verses in your Bible, reflect on them, journal about them, or write down any questions you have from your reading. We want to encourage you to take time to read God's love letter—the Bible. You'll find helpful tips in "How to Study the Bible on Your Own" (pages 115-117).

Option 3: Memory Verses

Memorizing Bible verses is an important habit to develop as you learn to grow spiritually on your own. "Memory Verses" (pages 118-119) contains six verses for you to memorize—one per session. Memorizing verses (and making them stick for more than a few minutes) isn't easy, but the benefits are undeniable. You'll have God's Word with you wherever you go.

> "I HAVE HIDDEN YOUR WORD IN MY HEART THAT I MIGHT NOT SIN AGAINST YOU." —PSALM 119:11

Option 4: Journaling

You'll find blank pages for journaling beginning on page 123. At the end of each session, you'll find questions to get your thoughts going—but you aren't limited to answering the questions listed. Use these pages to reflect, write a letter to God, note what you're learning, compose prayer, ask questions, draw pictures, record your thoughts, or take notes if your small group is using the EXPERIENCING CHRIST TOGETHER DVD teachings. For some suggestions about journaling, turn to "Journaling: Snapshots of Your Heart" on pages 120-122.

For this session, choose one or more questions to kickstart your journaling.

- I'm excited to be in a group because...
- If someone asked me to describe Jesus, I would say...
- Jesus would want me to know...

Of the five options listed here, mark the option(s) that seem most appealing to you. Share with your group the one(s) you plan to do in the upcoming week. This helps you keep one another accountable as you continue to study and grow on your own.

Option 5: Wrap It Up

Write out your answers to any questions that you didn't answer during your small group time.

LEARN A LITTLE MORE

Goal: To help you better understand the Scripture passage you studied in this session by highlighting key words and other important information.

If we drown (Mark 4:38)

Because the disciples were seasoned fishermen, they probably weren't just overreacting to this storm—it must have been a very dangerous one. The disciples use a strong word to describe their situation: apollumi. In Greek that means "to be fully destroyed." They may have really believed that this storm would kill them.

Sleeping on a cushion (4:38)

"The only place one could sleep in a small fishing boat with water pouring in from a storm would be on the elevated stern, where one could use the wooden or leather-covered helmsman's seat, or a pillow kept under that seat, as a cushion for one's head. Jesus' sleep during the storm may indicate the tranquility [peace] of faith (Psalm 4:8; cf. 2 Kings 6:16-17, 32; Proverbs 19:23)."[1]

No faith (4:40)

To Jesus, faith (trust) was very important, and this storm wasn't the only time that Jesus pointed out the disciples' lack of faith (see Mark 7:18; 8:17-18,21, 32-33; 9:19). These words ("no faith") indicate that the disciples should have been further along in their spiritual journeys than their fear showed. When our confidence in the One who can calm the storm is greater than our self-confidence, real faith happens.

The wind and the waves obey him (4:41)

Jesus is the Creator and Master over all created things, even the wind and sea. (See Psalm 65:5-13, 107:25,29 and Colossians 1:15-17.)

FOR DEEPER STUDY ON YOUR OWN

1. Check out the context for this passage by reading Mark 4:1-24. What did Jesus teach the disciples *before* he calmed the storm?

2. Check out these passages for Jesus' teaching about faith: Matthew 9:1-8, 14:22-33, and John 14:8-12.

3. What about Jesus does the Apostle Paul urge us to believe in Colossians 1:15-22? Why are these things so important to trust when we go through life's storms? What in this passage motivates you to surrender your worries to God?

---

[1]Keener, C. S., & InterVarsity Press, *The IVP Bible background commentary: New Testament* (Downers Grove, Ill.: InterVarsity Press, 1993) Mark 4:30.

A WEEKLY REFLECTION

Take a minute to reflect on how well you've been doing in the following five areas of your spiritual life this week—a 10 means you did an amazing job. This reflection can serve as a spiritual gauge to help you consider some very important areas. This is for your personal evaluation and growth; it's NOT a test—no one else needs to see it.

FELLOWSHIP: CONNECTING YOUR HEART TO OTHERS'

How well did I connect with other Christians?

1   2   3   4   5   6   7   8   9   10

DISCIPLESHIP: GROWING TO BE LIKE JESUS

How well did I take steps to grow spiritually and deepen my faith on my own?

1   2   3   4   5   6   7   8   9   10

MINISTRY: SERVING OTHERS IN LOVE

How well did I recognize opportunities to serve others and follow through?

1   2   3   4   5   6   7   8   9   10

EVANGELISM: SHARING YOUR STORY AND GOD'S STORY

How well did I engage in spiritual conversations with non-Christians?

1   2   3   4   5   6   7   8   9   10

WORSHIP: SURRENDERING YOUR LIFE TO HONOR GOD

How well did I focus on God's presence and honor him with my life? Was my relationship with God a primary focus?

1   2   3   4   5   6   7   8   9   10

When you finish, celebrate the areas where you feel good and consider how you can use those strengths to help others in their journey to be more like Jesus. You might also want to take time to identify some potential areas for growth.

THE KEY TO SIGNIFICANCE

 LEADERS, READ PAGE 82.

Natasha was an outstanding student. She worked hard to maintain straight As in her honors classes. She took pride in her accomplishments—from captaining the basketball team to winning a National Merit Scholarship. Natasha secretly loved it when her friends commented about how smart she was. During her senior year, she applied to several Ivy League universities. Yale was at the top of her list—and practically all she thought about.

One day Natasha's father came home from work and told the family he'd been laid off; Natasha's Ivy League dreams could be over. Natasha and her parents talked about other options for school—such as less expensive community colleges. But the idea of community college made her angry. Natasha felt robbed and thought that any other option was a complete waste. She became depressed and withdrew from her friends, too ashamed to tell even her best friends what was happening. What would they think? They all had the same plans and dreams.

At church one night Natasha finally opened up to her friend, Kristin. Kristin was planning to attend the local community college that fall, and she talked and prayed with Natasha—and opened up her eyes. Kristin had a learning disability that required her to work twice as hard—but without the amazing results Natasha experienced. Community college was Kristin's only option because it offered the special programs she needed to continue her education. As Kristin and Natasha continued to meet and pray each week, Natasha's disappointment lessened. She started to see that her true significance wasn't based on grades or attending a prestigious college. She learned a great life lesson—one more valuable than money could buy. In this session, we'll look at the meaning of true significance.

♥ FELLOWSHIP: CONNECTING YOUR HEART TO OTHERS'

Goal: To share about your life and listen attentively to others, caring about what they share

1. Share one thing in your life that you absolutely love.

2. What might happen if you lost that one thing?

DISCIPLESHIP: GROWING TO BE LIKE JESUS

Goal: To explore God's Word, gain biblical knowledge, and make personal applications

One thing we all have in common is the need for significance. We all want our lives to count, to make a difference in the world. But our quest for significance becomes problematic when we hold on too tightly to our dreams and fail to look at God's plan for each of us. We lose sight of the fact that God's way is always better than our way. True significance begins when we surrender our lives to God.

Jesus knew exactly how difficult this was—he surrendered

to his Father's plan, and it set him on a path toward a horrible death. Why did Jesus go through with it? Because he knew his Father had the best plan—and he was right!

Read John 12:23-33. (If you don't have a Bible, the passage is on page 90.)

1. What do you think it means for Jesus to be glorified?

2. What does the kernel illustration mean? What point was Jesus trying to make?

3. Suppose someone asked, "Maybe wheat has to die to produce more wheat, and maybe Jesus had to die in order to bring something priceless to the world, but why do I have to 'die' in order for my life to be significant?" How would you respond?

4. According to this passage, what is the key to eternal life?

5. What does it mean for a person to "love his life"?

6. Get personal: Have you ever loved this world too much? What are some areas in which you struggle?   *Boyfriend*
    School/social life (friends)
    Debate

7. Why is sacrifice so important? Why is sacrifice so powerful?

8. What does it mean to "hate" our lives? Aren't they gifts from God?

9. Why was Jesus' heart troubled? What does this say about who Jesus is—his character? How does verse 33 shed some light on this?

MINISTRY: SERVING OTHERS IN LOVE

Goal: To recognize and take advantage of opportunities to serve others

Surrender often means giving up or sacrificing something valuable. For example, a 10-year-old kid with a black belt in karate has given up a big chunk of childhood fun to reach that goal. Studying karate at such a high level also means a lot of sacrifice. Sacrifice and surrender are amazing acts.

1. Do you know someone who has fully surrendered his (or her) life to following Jesus?

2. Do you think this person is viewed as "a little weird" or "a Jesus freak"? Do you think this person may have experienced conflict because of his acts of sacrifice?

3. How might you and/or your small group show appreciation for someone who is totally committed to following God and his ways? Before you discuss what you could do, talk about why this person might need encouragement.

EVANGELISM: SHARING YOUR STORY AND GOD'S STORY

Goal: To consider how the truths from this session might be applied to your relationships with unbelievers

1. How does selfishness hurt our ability to be a witness to others?

2. Why is serving such a powerful way to reach out to non-Christians? What is one specific thing you could do this week to serve a non-Christian?

3. To a non-Christian, do you think a person surrendered to service is a positive or negative advertisement for Jesus? Explain your answer.

WORSHIP: SURRENDERING YOUR LIFE TO HONOR GOD

Goal: To focus on God's presence

Jesus knew that he was headed toward death, and he'd been warning his disciples about the costs of committing their lives to follow him.

1. What are some of the costs of following Jesus as a student?

2. Why do you believe each one is a cost? (Provide an answer for each cost you listed from the previous question.)

3. Read Luke 9:22-27, 57-62 (see page 91). What costs does Jesus promise here for following him?

4. Close in prayer and take your time to worship God by considering the costs of following him and fully surrendering to him.

AT HOME THIS WEEK

Option 1: A Weekly Reflection
Take another self-evaluation that reflects five areas of your spiritual life (fellowship, discipleship, ministry, evangelism, and worship). See pages 38-39.

Option 2: Daily Bible Readings
Check out the Bible reading plan on pages 113-114.

Option 3: Memory Verses
Memorize another verse from pages 118-119.

Option 4: Journaling

Choose one or more of the following options:

- Write down whatever is on your mind.

- Read your journal entry from last week and write a reflection about it.

- Answer these questions: What role does sacrifice play in my spiritual life? What would it take for others to describe me as someone who's a fully devoted follower of Jesus?

Option 5: Wrap It Up

Write out your answers to any questions that you didn't answer during your small group time.

LEARN A LITTLE MORE

Son of Man (John 12:23)

Jesus used this title for himself more than 80 times in the Gospels. It's significant for the following reasons: (1) Not only was Jesus divine (the "Son of God"), but he was also human; (2) His nationality was Jewish, but he also represented all humanity; (3) This term originated in the Old Testament, where it was used in reference to the promised Messiah (Psalm 80:17).

Be glorified (12:23)

Jesus spoke these words shortly before his arrest. He said his upcoming torture and death would reveal his divine glory (majesty). By our words and actions, we too can experience God's glory and magnificence and reveal it to others (John 12:28, 17:17-24).

"In John, crucifixion is described as glorification (7:39; 12:16, 23; 13:31; cf. 21:19)…It is an unveiling, a fresh radiating of God showing himself once more at work."[2]

[2]Green, J. B., McKnight, S., & Marshall, I. H., *Dictionary of Jesus and the Gospels* (Downers Grove, Ill.: InterVarsity Press, 1992) page 270.

Kernel of wheat...dies (12:24)

Technically speaking, when one plants a kernel of wheat, the seed doesn't die and later come back to life. In Jesus' symbolic language, he was saying that the seed must be buried (as the dead are) so it can be transformed into something new—a stalk of wheat. Jesus would die and then be transformed or glorified.

Loves his life...hates his life (12:25)

Jesus uses *love* and *hate* relatively. Compared to our passionate love and longing for eternal life, by rights we should hate the things that sustain only earthly life. Possessions, physical beauty, social status, and even health and well-being should be lower on our priority list than eternal things such as intimacy with God, love for others, and drawing others toward God. Even most Christians live as though earthly life is all there is, and earthly happiness is the highest goal. Jesus endured death because he knew earthly happiness isn't the point of life on earth—the point is that eternal life starts now! And eternal life is found only when we're willing to sacrifice and surrender what we cling to for earthly happiness.

We are on earth for such a short time. Yet if we use this time wisely, what we accomplish for Jesus in this life will last for eternity and be rewarded in eternity.

Prince of this world (12:31)

Satan is the ruler of this world (John 14:30, Ephesians 2:2). Although he was defeated by Jesus' death on the cross (John 16:11, 1 Corinthians 15:52-53), his ultimate defeat will come at the end of the world.

FOR DEEPER STUDY ON YOUR OWN

1. Read Matthew 10:37-39 for another of Jesus' teachings about the futility of loving the world.

2. In Philippians 2:6-11, check out how the world is going to respond to Jesus' glory at the end of time.

3. Look through these passages in John to learn more about Jesus' glorification: John 7:39; 12:16,23; 13:31.

4. The apostle Paul talked about losing and finding his life, too. Read Acts 22:1-22 and Philippians 3:4-14. What did Paul lose? What did he gain? Why couldn't he have gained those things and accomplished what he did without losing so much?

A WEEKLY REFLECTION

Take a minute to reflect on how well you've been doing in the following five areas of your spiritual life this week—a 10 means you did an amazing job. This reflection can serve as a spiritual gauge to help you consider some very important areas. This is for your personal evaluation and growth; it's NOT a test—no one else needs to see it.

FELLOWSHIP: CONNECTING YOUR HEART TO OTHERS'

How well did I connect with other Christians?

1   2   3   4   5   6   7   8   9   10

DISCIPLESHIP: GROWING TO BE LIKE JESUS

How well did I take steps to grow spiritually and deepen my faith on my own?

1   2   3   4   5   6   7   8   9   10

MINISTRY: SERVING OTHERS IN LOVE

How well did I recognize opportunities to serve others and follow through?

1   2   3   4   5   6   7   8   9   10

EVANGELISM: SHARING YOUR STORY AND GOD'S STORY

How well did I engage in spiritual conversations with non-Christians?

1   2   3   4   5   6   7   8   9   10

WORSHIP: SURRENDERING YOUR LIFE TO HONOR GOD

How well did I focus on God's presence and honor him with my life? Was my relationship with God a primary focus?

1   2   3   4   5   6   7   8   9   10

When you finish, celebrate the areas where you feel good and consider how you can use those strengths to help others in their journey to be more like Jesus. You might also want to take time to identify some potential areas for growth.

TRUE GREATNESS

 LEADERS, READ PAGE 82.

David was a *great* guy. He was a *great* student and *great* athlete. He had *great* friends and came from a *great* family. David's family wasn't merely *great*, it was unique. David was the oldest of four—and two of his younger brothers (twins) were born premature, and each had a unique birth defect. Kaleb was blind, and Caden had Down's syndrome.

David loved his siblings very much and made sacrifices for his family that most young people aren't asked to make. Medical bills were very steep, so both of David's parents worked. David was responsible for making sure his siblings were taken care of *before* school—then he had to race home to provide help *after* school. Instead of hanging out with friends, David read to his blind brother. Instead of playing sports, David was rolling a ball to his sister, Makayla. On the rare occasions he had free time, he didn't take it for himself; instead he'd take his brothers and sister to the movies. David's responsibilities were big for someone so young, but he loved it. David's life was different, and he knew it. He knew God had called him to live a different kind of *greatness*.

In this session we'll learn about what true greatness looks like.

♥ FELLOWSHIP: CONNECTING YOUR HEART TO OTHERS'

Goal: To share about your life and listen attentively to others, caring about what they share

1. From the list below, choose your favorite superhero and briefly explain your choice:

- Superman
- Batman
- Wonder Woman
- The Incredible Hulk
- Lara Croft
- Captain Marvel
- Spiderman
- The Flash
- Captain America
- Green Lantern
- Other:

DISCIPLESHIP: GROWING TO BE LIKE JESUS

Goal: To explore God's Word, gain biblical knowledge, and make personal applications

John the Baptist was a hero to many of Jesus' first disciples. He had a thriving ministry with national fame. He called the people of Israel to change their lives and turn to God's way (repentance), declaring that the kingdom of God was near. John the Baptist was such a "celebrity" that the religious leaders in Jerusalem sent an official group to find out if he saw himself as the Messiah—but he again pointed this group away from himself so their attention would be focused completely on Christ. In this session, we're going to take a look at John the Baptist so we can learn from his heroic example.

Read John 1:19-34. (If you don't have a Bible, the passage is on pages 91-92.)

1. Based upon this passage (and what you might have heard before), describe John the Baptist. Who was he? What did he do? What was his mission?

2. Why do you think the religious authorities may have thought John the Baptist was the promised Messiah?

3. How did John the Baptist prepare the people of Israel for the coming of Jesus?

4. How many times is the word *testimony* or *testify* used in this passage? What is John the Baptist's testimony? (Be specific and find your answers from the biblical text.)

5. John the Baptist's ministry was significant—he had a major impact on the people of Israel. Jesus said of him: "I tell you the truth: Among those born of women there has not risen anyone greater than John the Baptist..." (Matthew 11:11). In the midst of his success, how would you describe John the Baptist's attitude and heart?

6. Can ministry success ever turn into a bad thing? Explain your answer.

7. Consider successful ministry for a moment and—of the following statements—check the one you believe is wrong. Why do you feel this way?

- Christians are so good at helping others that they don't need God's help.
- I'm so busy doing God's work for others that I've missed out on God's work in me.
- All of my ministry skills, experience, and results mean I don't have to rely on God's Spirit that much.
- I help people a lot, so God helps me.

8. How did John the Baptist display humility in this passage?

9. Is there a difference between false humility and true humility? If so, what is it?

10. How would your attitude compare with John the Baptist's? Be honest, and explain why you feel the way you do.

MINISTRY: SERVING OTHERS IN LOVE

Goal: To recognize and take advantage of opportunities to serve others

Anyone fully surrendered to God exudes humility. Why? Because she understands God's greatness and recognizes her own humanity (and smallness). Her humility doesn't mean she believes she has no abilities to offer—rather, like John the Baptist, she looks for what God wants done in the world and then follows his lead, knowing he's in control. John the Baptist knew his job was to prepare people for Jesus, and he pursued that mission energetically and single-mindedly. Surrender for John didn't only mean giving up his own agenda, it meant being faithful to God's agenda.

1. Where do you see God at work around you? How might he want you to be involved in that work? What would that look like for you?

2. What gifts for service do you see in yourself?

3. How might you be tempted to seek status through serving others? What steps can you take to make sure you serve out of faithfulness rather than for status?

4. How can you let God increase while you decrease?

EVANGELISM: SHARING YOUR STORY AND GOD'S STORY

Goal: To consider how the truths from this session might be applied to your relationships with unbelievers

Arrogance is usually pretty easy to spot. Most of the time, arrogant people act as their own "cheerleaders." But arrogant people are usually hurting people, and their own cheerleading and the attention they get is often an attempt to heal the pain they feel inside. Arrogance isn't an attractive quality—it's a sign of weakness, not strength.

1. List a few ways you can spot an arrogant person.

2. How does an arrogant Christian defeat evangelism?

3. How would you confront a fellow Christian if you noticed pride, arrogance, or self-centeredness in his or her life? What would you say? Could you adequately explain your answer to the previous question?

WORSHIP: SURRENDERING YOUR LIFE TO HONOR GOD

Goal: To focus on God's presence

1. Are there any prayer requests you've shared with your group that you believe God has already answered? Share with the group.

2. Take a few minutes of silence and finish this thought: "God, I want to bring attention to you instead of me. I want to surrender my arrogance to you so that you are lifted up instead of me. I want to decrease so that you may increase. In order for this to happen, I need to make some changes in my life. Please help me with…" (See page 95 to record your prayer—"God, I want to bring attention to you…")

3. End your time by sharing how the group can pray for you and the things that need to change in your life, and then pray for each other.

AT HOME THIS WEEK

Option 1: A Weekly Reflection

Take another self-evaluation that reflects five areas of your spiritual life (fellowship, discipleship, ministry, evangelism, and worship). See pages 49-50.

Option 2: Daily Bible Readings

Check out the Bible reading plan on pages 113-114.

Option 3: Memory Verses

Memorize another verse from pages 118-119.

Option 4: Journaling

Choose one or more of the following options:

- Write down whatever is on your mind.
- Read your journal entry from last week and write a reflection about it.
- Finish these statements: I often want to be noticed because… For God to receive honor through my strengths, I need to…

Option 5: Wrap It Up

Write out your answers to any questions that you didn't answer during your small group time.

LEARN A LITTLE MORE

John (John 1:19)

John the Baptist was the greatest prophet the Jews had seen in centuries. He was known for baptizing (immersing in water) those who repented from their sins. Traditionally the Jews only gave "ritual baths" to pagan converts—the idea that Jews, too, needed to be cleansed from sin caused quite a stir for many in Israel.

I am not the Christ (1:20)

Many Jews were eagerly awaiting the Christ, the Savior-King they believed would overthrow the Romans and restore Israel as God's kingdom. The authorities in Jerusalem were quick to investigate anyone who might claim this title. Some of John's followers wanted him to proclaim himself the Christ, but John resisted that temptation because he knew there was someone greater coming.

Christ (1:20)

Christ is Greek for "anointed one" and is the equivalent of the Hebrew word *Messiah*. In the Old Testament, priests, kings, and prophets were anointed with oil (it was poured on their heads) as a symbol of God's blessing, selection, and authorization for a special purpose. Although many people were anointed, the Old Testament promised the coming of "the Anointed One"—the Messiah. During the time of Jesus, the Jews were waiting for God to send the Messiah to save them from physical bondage. Jesus did want to free the Jews from the Romans—but he was more concerned with their spiritual bondage. Because he didn't meet their expectations, many Jews didn't believe in him.

Elijah (1:21)

Elijah was an Old Testament prophet who performed many wonders in the name of God. The Bible says he was taken up to heaven in a chariot of fire, and among the Jews it was believed that Elijah would return. Jesus affirmed this belief in Mark 9:12.

Pharisees (1:24)

During the time of Jesus, the Pharisees were a powerful segment of Jewish society. They focused on bringing the Word of God to the people—in their homes—rather than focusing on worship in the temple. They accepted the entire Old Testament as inspired (not everyone did) and also considered oral tradition (teachings passed down from generation to generation) as equally authoritative. In the Gospels, the Pharisees are almost always cast in a negative light: "Their piety is attacked as hypocritical, their spiritual leadership is declared bankrupt, and they are charged with leading the nation to its doom."[3]

The Lamb of God (1:29)

John recognized that Jesus was the suffering servant prophesied in Isaiah 53:7. He would become the ultimate Passover lamb (Exodus 12:1-28), whose blood would deliver his people from eternal slavery and death (1 Peter 1:19).

FOR DEEPER STUDY ON YOUR OWN

1. Investigate John the Baptist's birth and ministry in Luke 1:5-25, 57-80; 3:1-20. What signs of his greatness do you see? What would you say was important to John the Baptist—and what wasn't important to him?

2. Check out what Jesus had to say about John the Baptist's ministry in Matthew 11:1-15.

[3] *Dictionary of Jesus and the Gospels* (Downers Grove, Ill.: InterVarsity Press, 1992)

3. Greatness is something everyone wants. Read Mark 10:35-45 to see what Jesus had to say about greatness.

4. Read Jesus' opinion of John the Baptist in Luke 7:28. What do you think Jesus meant? By what standard did Jesus measure greatness?

5. Luke 14:11 contains a saying Jesus repeated often. It's a core principle of God's kingdom. Why do you think God's kingdom operates like this?

A WEEKLY REFLECTION

Take a minute to reflect on how well you've been doing in the following five areas of your spiritual life this week—a 10 means you did an amazing job. This reflection can serve as a spiritual gauge to help you consider some very important areas. This is for your personal evaluation and growth; it's NOT a test—no one else needs to see it.

FELLOWSHIP: CONNECTING YOUR HEART TO OTHERS'
How well did I connect with other Christians?

1   2   3   4   5   6   7   8   9   10

DISCIPLESHIP: GROWING TO BE LIKE JESUS
How well did I take steps to grow spiritually and deepen my faith on my own?

1   2   3   4   5   6   7   8   9   10

MINISTRY: SERVING OTHERS IN LOVE

How well did I recognize opportunities to serve others and follow through?

1   2   3   4   5   6   7   8   9   10

EVANGELISM: SHARING YOUR STORY AND GOD'S STORY

How well did I engage in spiritual conversations with non-Christians?

1   2   3   4   5   6   7   8   9   10

WORSHIP: SURRENDERING YOUR LIFE TO HONOR GOD

How well did I focus on God's presence and honor him with my life? Was my relationship with God a primary focus?

1   2   3   4   5   6   7   8   9   10

When you finish, celebrate the areas where you feel good and consider how you can use those strengths to help others in their journey to be more like Jesus. You might also want to take time to identify some potential areas for growth.

SESSION 4
ATTITUDE OF GRATITUDE

 LEADERS, READ PAGE 82.

Karie was a high school student who felt God tugging at her heart one holiday season. Her family was well off and a wonderful Christmas was in store, with lots of presents and plenty of food. But when Karie thought about how good she had it, she began to think of those less fortunate. She knew they weren't only orphans in foreign countries (as she had seen on TV) but families in her own community...possibly even in her own neighborhood. She wanted to do something to help.

So Karie decided to act. She asked her family to use the money that would have been spent on her presents for grocery store gift certificates that she could give to a needy family. Her parents respected her conviction and agreed to give her $300 toward her plan. Karie bought the certificates and gave them to her church, which already knew of many families in need. As she made the donation, Karie felt grateful to have the opportunity to serve others in need.

Karie didn't know about Troy's family. His dad was out of a job, and Christmas was going to be miserable. Troy tried to hide their financial hardships from his friends at school and church. Any time his buddies did anything that cost money, he said he was too busy to join the fun. Troy knew that no one in his family would receive Christmas presents. He desperately wished he could help…but he didn't know what to do.

One Sunday after youth group, Troy's youth pastor asked him to stay and talk. He presented Troy with an anonymous gift. Troy went home and gave his family $300 worth of grocery store certificates, donated by a caring teenager.

♥ FELLOWSHIP: CONNECTING YOUR HEART TO OTHERS

Goal: To share about your life and listen attentively to others, caring about what they share

People who possess attitudes of gratitude live life with a different perspective. Because grateful people celebrate the little things they receive, they seem to live with a little more enthusiasm than those around them. Thankful people seem to understand God's goodness.

1. Name one thing you're grateful to God for.

2. Name one person you know who lives life with a grateful attitude.

3. Name one thing that gets in the way of your thankfulness.

DISCIPLESHIP: GROWING TO BE LIKE JESUS

Goal: To explore God's Word, gain biblical knowledge, and make personal applications

Surrendering to God requires sacrifice. Some sacrifices are so big that they defy human logic. God knows all about sacrifice, and he doesn't ask us to do anything he hasn't already done through Jesus. As you surrender your life to God, you'll see the continual need for sacrifice.

In this passage, you're going to learn about one person's extravagant sacrifice for Jesus. Though others misunderstood (and even criticized) this sacrificial act, Jesus appreciated it—because it was a pure expression of gratitude.

Read Mark 14:1-9. (If you don't have a Bible, the passage is on pages 92-93.)

1. Why do you think the religious leaders were concerned with arresting Jesus?

2. Retell this story in your own words.

3. What is the main teaching from these verses?

4. Why is the setting significant to this story?

5. Why did the woman put the perfume on Jesus' head?

6. Read verse 7 again. Since we'll always have the poor, does this mean we don't need to do anything to help them? Why, or why not? What do you think Jesus meant?

7. This woman faced harsh criticism for what she did. How do you let others' opinions influence the way you serve God and surrender to him?

8. Sometimes Christians are their own worst enemies. Do you ever criticize other Christians and the way they worship and serve God? (This is a tough one, but be honest!)

9. Let's put this event into perspective by looking at to-day's monetary situation. In Jesus' day, the entire jar of perfume cost a common laborer a year's wages. Today, if a person worked a 40-hour week at minimum wage, he would make more than $15,000 a year. Imagine this much money spent on one jar of perfume and then used (in its entirety, not just a little) on a poor rabbi's head. This image is one of extravagant worship and to-tal surrender to God. In your life—this week—what would it mean for you to surrender to God in such an extravagant manner?

MINISTRY: SERVING OTHERS IN LOVE

Goal: To recognize and take advantage of opportunities to serve others

It's not too difficult to go wild with gratitude for a brief period of time, such as an hour at church or youth group. Millions of people do it every week. You've seen them; they arrive at church and express their love to God—while they're in the building. Then they leave church and return to "normal" and express love for themselves throughout the week. For most Christians one hour a week doesn't equal sacrifice for God.

1. How can you help the people in your small group sustain gratitude toward Jesus all day long, day after day?

2. How can a small group become a place that encourages total surrender to God, consistent living, and an attitude of gratitude?

3. How would you grade yourself and your group in these areas?

EVANGELISM: SHARING YOUR STORY AND GOD'S STORY

Goal: To consider how the truths from this session might be applied to your relationships with unbelievers

Jesus made a bold statement in Mark 14:9: "I tell you the truth, wherever the gospel is preached throughout the world, what she has done will also be told, in memory of her."

1. Why do you think Jesus connects this event so closely with sharing the gospel?

2. How might non-Christians define extravagant worship of Jesus? Try to think of both positive and negative examples.

WORSHIP: SURRENDERING YOUR LIFE TO HONOR GOD

Goal: To focus on God's presence

1. In addition to dying on the cross, what has Jesus done that deserves your extravagant love, gratitude, and worship? Spend a minute and make a list below.

   – He has given me the ultimate best friend someone that will always be there.

2. Share something from your list with the group.

3. Take some time to write God a thank-you letter, using some of your answers from the previous questions as you construct it. You can write this letter on page 96.

4. In your closing prayer, focus only on thanking God for what he's done in your life. Write down each other's prayer requests and commit to pray for those throughout the week.

AT HOME THIS WEEK

Option 1: A Weekly Reflection

Take another self-evaluation that reflects five areas of your spiritual life (fellowship, discipleship, ministry, evangelism, and worship). See pages 58-59.

Option 2: Daily Bible Readings

Check out the Bible reading plan on pages 113-114.

Option 3: Memory Verses

Memorize another verse from pages 118-119.

Option 4: Journaling

Choose one or more of the following options:

- Write down whatever is on your mind.
- Read your journal entry from last week and write a reflection about it.
- Answer these questions: What needs to happen in my life so that I can become a more thankful person? Based on what I learned in this session, how does gratefulness increase my desire to surrender my life to God?

Option 5: Wrap It Up

Write out your answers to any questions that you didn't answer during your small group time.

LEARN A LITTLE MORE

Passover (Mark 14:1)

Passover is a ceremonial meal in which Jewish people remember how God protected their ancestors from a plague and freed them from Egyptian slavery (see Exodus 12:1-13:10). The plague was God's judgment on the Egyptians for Pharaoh's refusal to free the Israelites. It struck every firstborn child in Egypt, except those in homes where lamb's blood was spread on the doorposts. In an act of love and mercy, God "passed over" the Jewish homes marked with blood. To this day the Jews celebrate Passover by eating lamb and other special foods.

Jesus ate his last meal with his 12 disciples the evening before Passover. He used this meal to teach some key things about his mission and his desire for their future and the church's future. With bread and wine, Jesus taught them that his body (represented by the bread) and blood (the wine) would become the final Passover sacrifice. His death on the cross would free them from sin's spiritual slavery, and, by washing their feet, he taught them that his life and death were supreme acts of service, and that they should live their lives in this same manner.

Simon the Leper (14:3)

Simon's skin disease made him a social outcast. It was a great shock (and even an outrage) that Jesus would eat with such a person.

Pure nard (14:3)

The Jews anointed people to soften skin, heal the sick, welcome a guest, honor the dead, coronate kings, and consecrate priests. Instead of pouring just a little perfumed oil on Jesus' head, Mary used a whole pint of extremely costly oil. Jesus said she foresaw his coming need for burial ointment (John 12:7; compare with John 19:38-40.) The disciples at this point haven't come to grips with Jesus' prediction of his impending death.

A year's wages (14:5)

Literally, the text says "300 denarii." A single denarius was "the basic Roman silver coin used in Palestine...the average daily wage for a farm laborer."[1] One denarius was also the annual temple tax mentioned in Matthew 22:21.

FOR DEEPER STUDY ON YOUR OWN

1. A similar event is recorded in Luke 7:36-50. How is it similar to what Mary did in Bethany? How is it different?

2. In Ephesians 1:3-14, Paul praised God for a whole list of things God has done for us through Jesus. For which ones are you deeply grateful, and which ones do you perhaps take for granted or just not understand?

A WEEKLY REFLECTION

Take a minute to reflect on how well you've been doing in the following five areas of your spiritual life this week—a 10 means you did an amazing job. This reflection can serve as a spiritual gauge to help you consider some very important areas. This is for your personal evaluation and growth; it's NOT a test—no one else needs to see it.

FELLOWSHIP: CONNECTING YOUR HEART TO OTHERS'

How well did I connect with other Christians?

1   2   3   4   5   6   7   8   9   10

[1]Walvoord, J. F., Zuck, R. B., & Dallas Theological Seminary, *The Bible Knowledge Commentary : An Exposition of the Scriptures* (Wheaton, Ill.: Victor Books, 1983).

DISCIPLESHIP: GROWING TO BE LIKE JESUS

How well did I take steps to grow spiritually and deepen my faith on my own?

1   2   3   4   5   6   7   8   9   10

MINISTRY: SERVING OTHERS IN LOVE

How well did I recognize opportunities to serve others and follow through?

1   2   3   4   5   6   7   8   9   10

EVANGELISM: SHARING YOUR STORY AND GOD'S STORY

How well did I engage in spiritual conversations with non-Christians?

1   2   3   4   5   6   7   8   9   10

WORSHIP: SURRENDERING YOUR LIFE TO HONOR GOD

How well did I focus on God's presence and honor him with my life? Was my relationship with God a primary focus?

1   2   3   4   5   6   7   8   9   10

When you finish, celebrate the areas where you feel good and consider how you can use those strengths to help others in their journey to be more like Jesus. You might also want to take time to identify some potential areas for growth.

SESSION 5
ULTIMATE TRUST

 LEADERS, READ PAGE 82.

For the last three years, Chris has been in a rock band with several of his friends. He knew they had a great sound and a lot of potential. Chris and the other band members were passionate about music and loved playing together. During the last six months the band played many different venues ranging from friends' parties to community events and received a lot of exposure. With increased popularity came a larger time commitment and more pressure. But Chris didn't mind because he felt God had given him both the talent and the passion for music.

Unfortunately the more the band played together, the more Chris noticed the message in their music changing. What started as lyrically upbeat and positive became darker—even inappropriate. Chris went along with the shift because it seemed to be working; he didn't want to upset the other guys. As a matter of fact, it went so well that a friend's dad approached the band about signing a record contract! The band met a producer who liked their sound and asked them to submit a demo for the label executives.

All the guys in the band (except Chris) wanted to demo one song filled with sexual words and images. Chris began to wonder if his band's songs would begin moving in a more secular direction after signing this record contract. He was torn because getting his band signed was a gigantic opportunity—it was what he'd wanted ever since the band formed three years earlier. Chris felt stuck.

After a lot of prayer, time alone with God, seeking counsel from his small group, and sensing God's lead, Chris decided that the band wasn't moving in a direction that honored God. He tried to convince the other guys (who were also Christians—but not exactly focusing on their faith in the midst of all the excitement) to change direction, but they wanted to move forward with the new sound and didn't think it was a faith decision. Chris did, and he decided to leave the group.

Now Chris has to hang on to God's promise that he wants something better for Chris' life and music. It may not be what Chris expects, but he's confident that God will provide out of his goodness. Deep down Chris knows he made the right choice, regardless of what the future holds for the band and his friends in it.

♥ FELLOWSHIP: CONNECTING YOUR HEART TO OTHERS

Goal: To share about your life and listen attentively to others, caring about what they share

Trying to figure out God's will for your life can be difficult. In fact, it's sometimes easier to discern God's will in other people's lives than in your own! That's one of the beauties of a small group—your peers can help you understand God's will for your life. It's a great thing to be surrounded by friends who care.

1. What is one area of your life for which you wish you knew God's plan?

2. If you could ask God one question about your life, what would it be?

DISCIPLESHIP: GROWING TO BE LIKE JESUS

Goal: To explore God's Word, gain biblical knowledge, and make personal applications

Most of us will never face torture or death for our faith. But when we choose God's way, we will face moments when doing what God wants feels like torture. There are times when doing the right thing means venturing into the unknown, when doing God's will is costly. At those times, knowing that Jesus has been there, ahead of us, can make all the difference in the world.

In the passage you're about to discuss, you'll get an intimate look at one of Jesus' most tender and vulnerable moments. The night before his death, he prayed in preparation for his imminent torture and death on the cross. During this time, his closest friends (his disciples) seemed to abandon him while he was pursuing the will of his Father.

Read Matthew 26:36-46. (If you don't have a Bible, the passage is on page 93.)

1. Why was Jesus sad and troubled?

2. Why do you think Jesus took three friends with him to pray?

3. If Jesus is God, then why did he even need to pray?

4. Study Jesus' prayers in verses 39 and 42. What strikes you as significant in what he asks for and what's important to him?

5. Why is it important to you to know that surrendering to the Father's will wasn't always easy for Jesus?

6. What does it mean to trust God? Get practical and answer this as specifically as you can.

7. In your opinion, why would the disciples fall asleep when they knew how troubled Jesus was?

8. Describe a time when God was leading you to do something extremely difficult.

9. What does it mean that the "spirit is willing, but the body is weak"? According to verse 41, what can make temptation easier to avoid?

10. What's the difference between struggling with God's will and disobeying God's will? Where have you personally crossed that line?

MINISTRY: SERVING OTHERS IN LOVE

Goal: To recognize and take advantage of opportunities to serve others

Imagine this scenario: Your good friend (a follower of Jesus) is struggling over a decision about her future. She wants to make the right decision and stay centered on God's will.

1. How would you help your friend? What would you say?

2. Read Hebrews 4:15: "For we do not have a high priest [in Jesus] who is unable to sympathize with our weaknesses, but we have one who has been tempted in every way, just as we are—yet was without sin."

   How might you use the truth of this verse to encourage your struggling friend?

EVANGELISM: SHARING YOUR STORY AND GOD'S STORY

Goal: To consider how the truths from this session might be applied to your relationships with unbelievers

Throughout the EXPERIENCING CHRIST TOGETHER series, we've stressed that evangelism is more than preaching "at" people. Evangelism involves listening to others (and hearing their stories), being brave enough to share parts of your story (or "testimony"), and knowing enough about God's story to help others understand how much God loves them. Each component is an important part of evangelism.

1. How can you talk about pursuing God's will for your life when you share parts of your story?

2. How might a Christian wanting to do the right thing be attractive to a non-Christian? Do you think you're the type of Christian who makes pursuing God's will attractive to others? Explain your answer. If not, what do you think keeps you from becoming an attractive Christian?

🚶 WORSHIP: SURRENDERING YOUR LIFE TO HONOR GOD

Goal: To focus on God's presence

1. Imagine that you're one of Jesus' disciples on the night he went to pray in the Garden of Gethsemane. You've fallen asleep. When you wake up, you see Jesus. What would you say to him (other than "I'm sorry")?

2. What do you think Jesus would say to you about trusting God with your life? What could he say that would give you total confidence to surrender your life fully to following God's way?

3. Close your time by praying for each other, asking God to strengthen you to become Christians who actively pursue God's will.

AT HOME THIS WEEK

Option 1: A Weekly Reflection

Take another self-evaluation that reflects five areas of your spiritual life (fellowship, discipleship, ministry, evangelism, and worship). See pages 69-70.

Option 2: Daily Bible Readings

Check out the Bible reading plan on pages 113-114.

Option 3: Memory Verses

Memorize another verse from pages 118-119.

Option 4: Journaling

Choose one or more of the following options:

- Write down whatever is on your mind.
- Read your journal entry from last week and write a reflection about it.
- Respond to the following: Name a time in your life when you believed you knew God's will for your life. What makes total surrender a difficult concept for you to embrace?

Option 5: Wrap It Up

Write out your answers to any questions that you didn't answer during your small group time.

LEARN A LITTLE MORE

Gethsemane (Matthew 26:36)

In Hebrew, this word literally means "oil press," and it's the name for a garden near the Mount of Olives. It was located "across the Kidron Valley from Jerusalem and thus on the western slopes of the Mount of Olives."[1]

Two sons of Zebedee (26:37)

James and John (see Matthew 4:21).

This cup (26:39)

Jesus was talking about the cup of God's wrath (anger—see Isaiah 51:17,22; Jeremiah 25:15; Revelation 14:10, 16:19) that would be poured out on Jesus on the cross. God's wrath

[1]Achtemeier, P. J., Harper & Row, P., & Society of Biblical Literature. (1985). Harper's Bible Dictionary (San Francisco: Harper & Row, 1985) page XX.

is the punishment for our sin. But because "God made him who had no sin to be sin for us" (2 Corinthians 5:21), Jesus bore God's wrath in our place.

Jesus knew what he was about to face: REAL suffering, REAL pain, REAL agony. It wasn't fake, nor was it an easy burden to carry. Jesus didn't relish dying on the cross by any stretch—he even asked his Father, "…if it is possible take this away from me…"

The spirit is willing, but the body is weak (26:41)

The disciples had surrendered, but only up to the point where their bodies and instincts screamed, "No!" Jesus modeled for them how to withstand the instinct to run from pain. Prayer kept Jesus grounded in the Father. After his resurrection, his disciples learned to do the same.

FOR DEEPER STUDY ON YOUR OWN

1. Read what Mark and Luke have to say about Jesus' prayer in the garden in Mark 14:32-42 and Luke 22:39-46.

2. Read Proverbs 3:5-6 to see what it means to trust God.

3. Check out 2 Corinthians 12:7-11 to learn about Paul's struggles, and how God used him in spite of his weakness.

4. Jesus quoted Psalm 22:1 on the cross. How does the psalmist deal with suffering and sorrow in Psalm 22?

5. Examine the attitudes toward the Father that Jesus said should shape the way we pray (Matthew 7:7-12). How do you see these attitudes at work in Jesus' prayers in Matthew 26?

A WEEKLY REFLECTION

Take a minute to reflect on how well you've been doing in the following five areas of your spiritual life this week—a 10 means you did an amazing job. This reflection can serve as a spiritual gauge to help you consider some very important areas. This is for your personal evaluation and growth; it's NOT a test—no one else needs to see it.

FELLOWSHIP: CONNECTING YOUR HEART TO OTHERS'

How well did I connect with other Christians?

1   2   3   4   5   6   7   8   9   10

DISCIPLESHIP: GROWING TO BE LIKE JESUS

How well did I take steps to grow spiritually and deepen my faith on my own?

1   2   3   4   5   6   7   8   9   10

MINISTRY: SERVING OTHERS IN LOVE

How well did I recognize opportunities to serve others and follow through?

1   2   3   4   5   6   7   8   9   10

EVANGELISM: SHARING YOUR STORY AND GOD'S STORY

How well did I engage in spiritual conversations with non-Christians?

1   2   3   4   5   6   7   8   9   10

WORSHIP: SURRENDERING YOUR LIFE TO HONOR GOD

How well did I focus on God's presence and honor him with my life? Was my relationship with God a primary focus?

1   2   3   4   5   6   7   8   9   10

When you finish, celebrate the areas where you feel good and consider how you can use those strengths to help others in their journey to be more like Jesus. You might also want to take time to identify some potential areas for growth.

SESSION 6

VICTORY OVER DEATH

 LEADERS, READ PAGE 82.

You can tell a lot about a person by the way he or she dies.

Pablo Picasso was one of greatest painters of the 20th century. He was perhaps the chief inventor of modern art. You might expect that at the end of his life, he would be thrilled with his incredible accomplishments—but he wasn't! In fact, as Picasso's body began to give way to illness, he painted with more and more frenzy. In the face of death, all his previous work seemed useless to him, and he became driven to paint *the* painting—his masterpiece. He filled his house with beautiful paintings, but with every non-masterpiece painting, the more frantically Picasso painted until he died.[4]

How different from the death of William Wilberforce in 1833. He spent decades campaigning to abolish slavery in the British Empire, and even as his health failed, he continued to do everything he could. He hoped he would stay alive long enough to see the slaves freed. Neither his letters nor his friends' comments reflect a life of frenzy or anxiety. When the

[4] The contrast between Picasso and Wilberforce is noted by *Os Guinness in Entrepreneurs of Life: Faith and the Venture of Purposeful Living* (Colorado Springs, Colo.: NavPress, 2001), pages 204-13.

slavery was finally outlawed, Wilberforce thanked God with joy. Two days later, his health began to fail rapidly, and on the third day he died.

Wilberforce persevered because he had eternity in mind. Picasso was driven crazy because he saw death as rendering life pointless and futile. If we want to live with perseverance and joy rather than emptiness and despair, we need only Jesus' example.

♥ FELLOWSHIP: CONNECTING YOUR HEART TO OTHERS'

Goal: To share about your life and listen attentively to others, caring about what they share

It's odd to think about death, especially when you're young— it's typically many, many years away. But thinking about death can teach us a lot about life. And when you understand what's after death for you, it can make living for today so much more rewarding.

If you knew you were going to die one year from today, how would you live your final year? How about one month from today? One week? One day?

DISCIPLESHIP: GROWING TO BE LIKE JESUS

Goal: To explore God's Word, gain biblical knowledge, and make personal applications

The backbone of the Christian faith is the resurrection of Jesus. Paul wrote, "And if Christ has not been raised, our preaching is useless and so is your faith" (1 Corinthians 15:14).

During his earthly ministry, Jesus predicted that he would be killed, and that he would defeat death through resurrection (Mark 10:32-34). Jesus taught many shocking truths and even claimed to be God. But his teachings weren't fairy tales—his resurrection proves everything he taught and did is true. While Jesus proved a lot through his miracles, skeptics discounted many of them. Jesus is the only person who has defeated death by rising from the dead. Because of Jesus' resurrection, Christians' physical deaths will be different as well—they won't ring with finality: "Where, O death, is your victory? Where, O death, is your sting?" (1 Corinthians 15:55).

We worship a crucified Savior who died to free us from our sin and offers us eternal life after death. We also worship a resurrected and living Lord. Because of that, total surrender of our lives is safe, because he is alive, and we, too, will live forever.

Read Matthew 28:1–20. (If you don't have a Bible, the passage is on page 94.)

1. What role do women play in this passage, and how is this significant?

2. In your opinion, why did people respond in fear to the angel?

3. Matthew is very careful to give us a detailed account. Reread this passage and point out the details you think are important to Jesus' victory over death.

4. As the women left the tomb in verse 8, they were filled with fear and joy. How can you explain this? Aren't these opposite feelings?

5. What lie did the Jewish leaders start?

6. What motivated the guards to keep their secret?

7. Why is it significant that Jesus defeated death? Wouldn't it have been enough if he just died for our sins?

8. When Jesus appeared to his disciples, why did he talk about his authority? Wouldn't his disciples already have recognized his authority?

9. According to the last two verses in this passage, what did Jesus command his disciples to do?

10. Of these commands, which are you best at? Which one needs some work?

MINISTRY: SERVING OTHERS IN LOVE

Goal: To recognize and take advantage of opportunities to serve others

Jesus came to die on the cross and defeat death so we could have access to God and develop an intimate relationship with him.

1. What is your mission? If you're not sure, what are some things you're passionate about?

2. If you're not sure about your mission, what is something you could do to discover it? If you think you have an idea about your mission, what is something you could do this week to express or confirm God's call in your life?

EVANGELISM: SHARING YOUR STORY AND GOD'S STORY

Goal: To consider how the truths from this session might be applied to your relationships with unbelievers

Many of Jesus' disciples faced torture and execution because of their confidence that Jesus defeated death through his resurrection. They saw firsthand that the gospel message was real, and so they were freed from their fear of death. What Jesus said would happen actually happened—he rose from the grave!

1. If you had total confidence (no doubts) that Jesus did what he said he did, how would that confidence affect your testimony about Jesus?

2. What kind of information do you need to feel more confident in the validity of the resurrection? Do you think non-Christians care about research related to the resurrection? How would you use this information carefully when talking to non-Christians?

WORSHIP: SURRENDERING YOUR LIFE TO HONOR GOD

Goal: To focus on God's presence

This final section is a time to celebrate where you've been together and where you're going as a small group. But before you talk about what's next for your group, make sure you end your time together by thinking about what Jesus did on the cross for you and how that ultimate sacrifice can lead to a surrendered life.

Imagine that you really, really know you're going to live forever in heaven because you're a Christian (actually, you may not need to imagine it—you may be confident in that teaching—which is great). You understand that health problems and disabilities are temporary. You know that failure isn't final because Jesus defeated death on the cross, and you were meant to live forever. Can you imagine that?

1. How should that belief affect the way you live now— especially your willingness to surrender completely?

2. Have you surrendered yourself to God more deeply in some area as a result of this small group? If so, share as much about that act of surrender with the group as you are willing to share.

Since this is the last time your group will be together with this particular book as your guide, make sure you take some time to discuss what will happen to your group next. If you want to continue to study the incredible life and teachings of Jesus, there are a total of six books in this series.

3. Look back at your prayer requests over the weeks you've been together. What answers to prayer have you heard and seen? Give thanks for answered prayers and for the growth you've experienced through this group.

4. Close your time by worshipping God through prayer.

AT HOME THIS WEEK

Option 1: A Weekly Reflection

Take another self-evaluation that reflects five areas of your spiritual life (fellowship, discipleship, ministry, evangelism, and worship). See pages 78-79.

Option 2: Daily Bible Readings

Check out the Bible reading plan on pages 113-114.

Option 3: Memory Verses

Memorize another verse from pages 118-119.

Option 4: Journaling

Choose one or more of the following options:

- Write down whatever is on your mind.
- Read your journal entry from last week and write a reflection about it.
- Answer these questions: How can I really know that Jesus rose from the dead? How does the hope of eternal life with God shape the way I view my life today?

Option 5: Wrap It Up

Write out your answers to any questions that you didn't answer during your small group time.

LEARN A LITTLE MORE

Mary Magdalene and the other Mary (Matthew 28:1)

Mary Magdalene is mentioned first in every listing of Jesus' female "disciples." According to all four Gospels, she witnessed Jesus death, was present at the empty tomb, saw the risen Lord, and received news to tell the disciples. The other Mary was "Mary the mother of James and John" (Matthew 27:56).

Sabbath (28:1)

God created the earth in seven days; he worked for six days and rested (literally, he "ceased") on the seventh day. God did this as a model for us to follow. He doesn't need the rest, but we do. It seems that the reason behind the Sabbath is for people to stop and take "time out" from their busy lives to focus on God. For many Jews, the Sabbath is a celebration, spent in prayer and with the family. Out of a misguided desire to observe the Sabbath as God intended, many of the Jewish leaders of Jesus' day created hundreds of rules governing conduct. These detailed rules were derived from Scripture, but were closer to human tradition, not God's revelation.

Guards (28:4)

The authorities placed Roman guards at Jesus' tomb in order to make sure that nobody stole the body and claimed Jesus had risen from the dead (Matthew 27:62-66).

Disciples (28:16)

The word *disciple* means learner or student and refers to a person who accepts the beliefs and teachings of a specific teacher. A committed disciple is devoted not only to learning, but also to living out the instructions of the teacher. In the New Testament, disciple usually refers to a follower of Jesus (sometimes just his 12 closest disciples; at other times to the many who followed Jesus). *Disciple* in the New Testament covers a range of commitment levels; however, Jesus often painted a clear picture of what it meant to be a true disciple (see Matthew 16:24-26).

FOR DEEPER STUDY ON YOUR OWN

1. Read Luke 24:1-53 for other encounters people had with Jesus after the resurrection. See 1 Corinthians 15:3-8 for a list of the people Jesus appeared to after the resurrection.

2. Thomas, one of the 12 disciples, had a lot of doubts about Jesus. Check out John 20:24-29 to see how Jesus reassured Thomas in his doubt.

3. What did Paul say the resurrection demonstrates in Romans 1:4? How does that fact affect you personally?

4. How is the Christian belief in bodily resurrection different from the belief that souls are immortal (1 Corinthians 15:35-54)? How is it different from reincarnation? Why does it matter that Jesus was raised bodily and didn't just return as a spirit?

5. How does Jesus' resurrection affect your relationship to sin (Romans 6:1-14)?

A WEEKLY REFLECTION

Take a minute to reflect on how well you've been doing in the following five areas of your spiritual life this week—a 10 means you did an amazing job. This reflection can serve as a spiritual gauge to help you consider some very important areas. This is for your personal evaluation and growth; it's NOT a test—no one else needs to see it.

FELLOWSHIP: CONNECTING YOUR HEART TO OTHERS'

How well did I connect with other Christians?

1   2   3   4   5   6   7   8   9   10

DISCIPLESHIP: GROWING TO BE LIKE JESUS

How well did I take steps to grow spiritually and deepen my faith on my own?

1   2   3   4   5   6   7   8   9   10

MINISTRY: SERVING OTHERS IN LOVE

How well did I recognize opportunities to serve others and follow through?

1   2   3   4   5   6   7   8   9   10

EVANGELISM: SHARING YOUR STORY AND GOD'S STORY

How well did I engage in spiritual conversations with non-Christians?

1   2   3   4   5   6   7   8   9   10

WORSHIP: SURRENDERING YOUR LIFE TO HONOR GOD

How well did I focus on God's presence and honor him with my life? Was my relationship with God a primary focus?

1   2   3   4   5   6   7   8   9   10

When you finish, celebrate the areas where you feel good and consider how you can use those strengths to help others in their journey to be more like Jesus. You might also want to take time to identify some potential areas for growth.

APPENDICES

SMALL GROUP LEADER CHECKLIST

- **Read through "For Small Group Leaders: How to Best Use this Material"** (see pages 83-86). This is very important—familiarizing yourself with it will help you understand content and how to best manage your time.

- **Read through all the questions in the session that you'll be leading.** The questions are a guide for you to help students grow spiritually. Think through which questions are best for your group. Remember, no curriculum author knows your students better than you do! Just a small amount of preparation on your part will help you manage the time you'll have with your group. Based on the amount of time you'll have in your small group, circle the questions you will discuss as a group. Decide what (if anything) you will assign at the end of the session (things like homework, snacks, group project, and so on).

- **Remember that the questions in this book don't always have obvious, neat, tidy answers.** Some are purposely written to cause good discussion without a specific "right" answer. Often questions (and answers) will lead to more questions.

- **Make sure you have enough books for your students and a few extra in case your students invite friends.** (Note: It's vital for your group to decide during the first session whether you can invite friends to join your group. If not, encourage your group to think of friends they can invite if you go through the next EXPERIENCING CHRIST TOGETHER book in this series.)

- **Read the material included in this appendix.** It's filled with information that will benefit your group and your student ministry. This appendix alone is a great reference for students—familiarize yourself with the tools here so you can offer them to students.

- **Submit your leadership and your group to God.** Ask God to provide you with insight into how to lead your group, patience to do so, and courage to speak truth in love when needed.

FOR SMALL GROUP LEADERS: HOW TO BEST USE THIS MATERIAL

This book was written more as a guidebook than a workbook. In most workbooks, you're supposed to answer every question and fill in all the blanks. In this book, there are lots of questions and plenty of blank space. Explain to your students that this isn't a school workbook—they're not graded on how much they've written.

The number-one rule for this curriculum is that there are no rules apart from the ones you decide to use. Every small group is unique and will figure out its own style and system. (The exception is when the lead youth worker establishes a guideline for all the groups to follow. In that case, respect your leader's guidelines.)

If you need a guide to get you started until you navigate your own way, here's a way to adapt the material for a 60-minute session.

Introduction (4 minutes)

Begin each session with one student reading the Small Group Covenant (see page 18). This becomes a constant reminder of why you'll be doing what you're doing. Then have another student read the opening paragraphs of the session you'll be discussing. Allow different students to take turns reading these two opening pieces.

Connecting (10 minutes)

This section can take 45 minutes if you're not careful! You'll need to stay on task to keep this segment short—consider giving students a specific amount of time and holding them to it. It's always better to leave students wanting more time for discussion than to leave them bored.

Growing (25 minutes)

Read God's Word and work through the questions you think will be best for your group. This section definitely has more questions than you're able to discuss in the allotted time. Before the small group begins, take some time to read through the questions and choose the best ones for your group. You may also want to add questions of your own. If someone forgets a Bible, we've provided the Scripture passages for each session in the appendix.

The questions in this book don't always have obvious, neat, tidy answers. Some are purposely written to cause good discussion without a specific "right" answer. Often questions (and answers) will lead to more questions.

If your small group is biblically mature, this section won't be too difficult. However, if your group struggles with these questions, make sure you sift through them and focus on the few questions that will help drive the message home. Also, you might want to encourage your group to answer the remaining questions on their own.

Serving and Sharing (10 minutes)

If you're pressed for time, you may choose to skip one of these two sections. If you do need to skip one due to time constraints, group members can finish the section on their own during the week. Don't feel guilty about passing over a section. **One of the strengths of this material is the built-in, intentional repetition in every session. You will have other opportunities to discuss that biblical purpose.** (Again, that's the main reason for spending a few minutes before your group meets to read through all the questions and pick the best ones for your group.)

Surrendering (10 minutes)

We always want to end the lesson with a focus on God and a specific time of prayer. You'll have several options but feel free to default to your group's comfort level.

Closing Challenge (1 minute)

Encourage students to pick one option each from the "At Home This Week" section to complete on their own. The more students initiate and develop the habit of spending time with God, the healthier their spiritual journeys will be. We've found that students have plenty of unanswered questions that they will consider on their own time. **Keep in mind that the main goal of this book is building spiritual growth in community—not to get your students to answer every question correctly.** Remember that this is your small group, your time, and the questions will always be there. Use them, ignore them, or assign them for personal study during the week—but don't feel pressure to follow this curriculum exactly or "grade" your group's biblical knowledge.

Finally, remember that questions are a great way to get students connected to one another and God's Word. You don't have to have all the answers.

Suggestions for Existing Small Groups

If your small group has been meeting for a while, and you've already established comfortable relationships, you can jump right into the material. But make sure you take the following actions, even if you're a well-established group:

- Read through the "Small Group Covenant" on page 18 and make additions or adjustments as necessary.

- Read the "Prayer Request Guidelines" together (pages 131-132). You can maximize the group's time by following them.

- Before each meeting, consider whether you'll assign material to be completed (or at least thought through) before your next meeting.

- Familiarize yourself with all the "At Home This Week" options at the end of each session. They are explained in detail near the end of Session 1 (pages 25-27), and then briefly summarized at the end of the other five sessions.

Although handling business like this can seem cumbersome or unnecessary to an existing group, these foundational steps can save you from headaches later on because you took the time to create an environment conducive to establishing deep relationships.

Suggestions for New Small Groups

If your group is meeting together for the first time, jumping right into the first session may not be your best option. You may want to meet as a group before you begin going through the book so you can get to know each other better. To prepare for the first gathering, read and follow the "Suggestions for Existing Groups" mentioned previously.

Spend some time getting to know each other with icebreaker questions. Several are listed here. Pick one or two that will work best for your group or use your own. The goal is to break ground so you can plant the seeds of healthy relationships.

1. What's your name, school, grade, and favorite class in school? (Picking your least favorite class is too easy.)

2. Tell the group a brief (basic) history of your family. What's your family life like? How many brothers and sisters do you have? Which family members are you closest to?

3. What's one thing about yourself that you really like?

4. Everyone has little personality quirks—traits that make each one of us unique. What are yours?

5. Why did you choose to be a part of this small group?

6. What do you hope to get out of this small group? How do you expect it to help you?

7. What do you think it will take to make our small group work well?

Need some teaching help?

Companion DVDs are available for each EXPERIENCING CHRIST TOGETHER book. These DVDs contain teaching segments you can use to supplement each session. Play them before your discussion begins or just prior to the "Discipleship" section in each session. The DVDs aren't required, but they are a great complement and supplement to the small group material. These are available from www.youthspecialties.com.

SCRIPTURE PASSAGES

Session 1

Mark 4:35-41

³⁵That day when evening came, he said to his disciples, "Let us go over to the other side." ³⁶Leaving the crowd behind, they took him along, just as he was, in the boat. There were also other boats with him. ³⁷A furious squall came up, and the waves broke over the boat, so that it was nearly swamped. ³⁸Jesus was in the stern, sleeping on a cushion. The disciples woke him and said to him, "Teacher, don't you care if we drown?"

³⁹He got up, rebuked the wind and said to the waves, "Quiet! Be still!" Then the wind died down and it was completely calm.

⁴⁰He said to his disciples, "Why are you so afraid? Do you still have no faith?"

⁴¹They were terrified and asked each other, "Who is this? Even the wind and the waves obey him!"

Psalm 31:1-24

¹In you, O Lord, I have taken refuge;

   let me never be put to shame;

   deliver me in your righteousness.

²Turn your ear to me,

   come quickly to my rescue;

be my rock of refuge,

   a strong fortress to save me.

³Since you are my rock and my fortress,

   for the sake of your name lead and guide me.

⁴Free me from the trap that is set for me,

   for you are my refuge.

⁵Into your hands I commit my spirit;

   redeem me, O Lord, the God of truth.

⁶I hate those who cling to worthless idols;

   I trust in the Lord.

⁷I will be glad and rejoice in your love,

   for you saw my affliction

   and knew the anguish of my soul.

⁸You have not handed me over to the enemy

   but have set my feet in a spacious place.

⁹Be merciful to me, O Lord, for I am in distress;

   my eyes grow weak with sorrow,

   my soul and my body with grief.

¹⁰My life is consumed by anguish

   and my years by groaning;

   my strength fails because of my affliction,

   and my bones grow weak.

¹¹Because of all my enemies,

   I am the utter contempt of my neighbors;

   I am a dread to my friends—

   those who see me on the street flee from me.

¹²I am forgotten by them as though I were dead;

   I have become like broken pottery.

¹³For I hear the slander of many;

   there is terror on every side;

   they conspire against me

   and plot to take my life.

¹⁴But I trust in you, O Lord;

I say, "You are my God."

¹⁵My times are in your hands;

deliver me from my enemies

and from those who pursue me.

¹⁶Let your face shine on your servant;

save me in your unfailing love.

¹⁷Let me not be put to shame, O Lord,

for I have cried out to you;

but let the wicked be put to shame

and lie silent in the grave.

¹⁸Let their lying lips be silenced,

for with pride and contempt

they speak arrogantly against the righteous.

¹⁹How great is your goodness,

which you have stored up for those who fear you,

which you bestow in the sight of men

on those who take refuge in you.

²⁰In the shelter of your presence you hide them

from the intrigues of men;

in your dwelling you keep them safe

from accusing tongues.

²¹Praise be to the Lord,

for he showed his wonderful love to me

when I was in a besieged city.

^{22}In my alarm I said,

"I am cut off from your sight!"

Yet you heard my cry for mercy

when I called to you for help.

^{23}Love the Lord, all his saints!

The Lord preserves the faithful,

but the proud he pays back in full.

^{24}Be strong and take heart,

all you who hope in the Lord.

Session 2

John 12:23-33

^{23}Jesus replied, "The hour has come for the Son of Man to be glorified. ^{24}I tell you the truth, unless a kernel of wheat falls to the ground and dies, it remains only a single seed. But if it dies, it produces many seeds. ^{25}The man who loves his life will lose it, while the man who hates his life in this world will keep it for eternal life. ^{26}Whoever serves me must follow me; and where I am, my servant also will be. My Father will honor the one who serves me.

^{27}"Now my heart is troubled, and what shall I say? 'Father, save me from this hour'? No, it was for this very reason I came to this hour. ^{28}Father, glorify your name!"

Then a voice came from heaven, "I have glorified it, and will glorify it again." ^{29}The crowd that was there and heard it said it had thundered; others said an angel had spoken to him.

^{30}Jesus said, "This voice was for your benefit, not mine. ^{31}Now is the time for judgment on this world; now the prince of this world will be driven out. ^{32}But I, when I am lifted up from the earth, will draw all men to myself." ^{33}He said this to show the kind of death he was going to die.

Luke 9:22-27

[22]And he said, "The Son of Man must suffer many things and be rejected by the elders, chief priests and teachers of the law, and he must be killed and on the third day be raised to life."

[23]Then he said to them all: "If anyone would come after me, he must deny himself and take up his cross daily and follow me. [24]For whoever wants to save his life will lose it, but whoever loses his life for me will save it. [25]What good is it for a man to gain the whole world, and yet lose or forfeit his very self? [26]If anyone is ashamed of me and my words, the Son of Man will be ashamed of him when he comes in his glory and in the glory of the Father and of the holy angels. [27]I tell you the truth, some who are standing here will not taste death before they see the kingdom of God."

Luke 9:57-62

[57]As they were walking along the road, a man said to him, "I will follow you wherever you go."

[58]Jesus replied, "Foxes have holes and birds of the air have nests, but the Son of Man has no place to lay his head."

[59]He said to another man, "Follow me."

But the man replied, "Lord, first let me go and bury my father."

[60]Jesus said to him, "Let the dead bury their own dead, but you go and proclaim the kingdom of God."

[61]Still another said, "I will follow you, Lord; but first let me go back and say good-bye to my family."

[62]Jesus replied, "No one who puts his hand to the plow and looks back is fit for service in the kingdom of God."

Session 3

John 1:19-34

[19]Now this was John's testimony when the Jews of Jerusalem sent priests and Levites to ask him who he was. [20]He did not fail to confess, but confessed freely, "I am not the Christ."

[21]They asked him, "Then who are you? Are you Elijah?"

He said, "I am not."

"Are you the Prophet?"

He answered, "No."

22Finally they said, "Who are you? Give us an answer to take back to those who sent us. What do you say about yourself?"

23John replied in the words of Isaiah the prophet, "I am the voice of one calling in the desert, 'Make straight the way for the Lord.'"

24Now some Pharisees who had been sent 25questioned him, "Why then do you baptize if you are not the Christ, nor Elijah, nor the Prophet?"

26"I baptize with water," John replied, "but among you stands one you do not know. 27He is the one who comes after me, the thongs of whose sandals I am not worthy to untie."

28This all happened at Bethany on the other side of the Jordan, where John was baptizing.

29The next day John saw Jesus coming toward him and said, "Look, the Lamb of God, who takes away the sin of the world! 30This is the one I meant when I said, 'A man who comes after me has surpassed me because he was before me.' 31I myself did not know him, but the reason I came baptizing with water was that he might be revealed to Israel."

32Then John gave this testimony: "I saw the Spirit come down from heaven as a dove and remain on him. 33I would not have known him, except that the one who sent me to baptize with water told me, 'The man on whom you see the Spirit come down and remain is he who will baptize with the Holy Spirit.' 34I have seen and I testify that this is the Son of God."

Session 4

Mark 14:1-9

1Now the Passover and the Feast of Unleavened Bread were only two days away, and the chief priests and the teachers of the law were looking for some sly way to arrest Jesus and kill him. 2"But not during the Feast," they said, "or the people may riot."

3While he was in Bethany, reclining at the table in the home of a man known as Simon the Leper, a woman came with an alabaster jar of very expensive perfume, made of pure nard. She broke the jar and poured the perfume on his head.

⁴Some of those present were saying indignantly to one another, "Why this waste of perfume? ⁵It could have been sold for more than a year's wages and the money given to the poor." And they rebuked her harshly.

⁶"Leave her alone," said Jesus. "Why are you bothering her? She has done a beautiful thing to me. ⁷The poor you will always have with you, and you can help them any time you want. But you will not always have me. ⁸She did what she could. She poured perfume on my body beforehand to prepare for my burial. ⁹I tell you the truth, wherever the gospel is preached throughout the world, what she has done will also be told, in memory of her."

Session 5

Matthew 26:36-46

³⁶Then Jesus went with his disciples to a place called Gethsemane, and he said to them, "Sit here while I go over there and pray." ³⁷He took Peter and the two sons of Zebedee along with him, and he began to be sorrowful and troubled. ³⁸Then he said to them, "My soul is overwhelmed with sorrow to the point of death. Stay here and keep watch with me."

³⁹Going a little farther, he fell with his face to the ground and prayed, "My Father, if it is possible, may this cup be taken from me. Yet not as I will, but as you will."

⁴⁰Then he returned to his disciples and found them sleeping. "Could you men not keep watch with me for one hour?" he asked Peter. ⁴¹"Watch and pray so that you will not fall into temptation. The spirit is willing, but the body is weak."

⁴²He went away a second time and prayed, "My Father, if it is not possible for this cup to be taken away unless I drink it, may your will be done."

⁴³When he came back, he again found them sleeping, because their eyes were heavy. ⁴⁴So he left them and went away once more and prayed the third time, saying the same thing.

⁴⁵Then he returned to the disciples and said to them, "Are you still sleeping and resting? Look, the hour is near, and the Son of Man is betrayed into the hands of sinners. ⁴⁶Rise, let us go! Here comes my betrayer!"

Session 6

Matthew 28:1-20

[1]After the Sabbath, at dawn on the first day of the week, Mary Magdalene and the other Mary went to look at the tomb.

[2]There was a violent earthquake, for an angel of the Lord came down from heaven and, going to the tomb, rolled back the stone and sat on it. [3]His appearance was like lightning, and his clothes were white as snow. [4]The guards were so afraid of him that they shook and became like dead men.

[5]The angel said to the women, "Do not be afraid, for I know that you are looking for Jesus, who was crucified. [6]He is not here; he has risen, just as he said. Come and see the place where he lay. [7]Then go quickly and tell his disciples: 'He has risen from the dead and is going ahead of you into Galilee. There you will see him.' Now I have told you."

[8]So the women hurried away from the tomb, afraid yet filled with joy, and ran to tell his disciples. [9]Suddenly Jesus met them. "Greetings," he said. They came to him, clasped his feet and worshiped him. [10]Then Jesus said to them, "Do not be afraid. Go and tell my brothers to go to Galilee; there they will see me."

[11]While the women were on their way, some of the guards went into the city and reported to the chief priests everything that had happened. [12]When the chief priests had met with the elders and devised a plan, they gave the soldiers a large sum of money, [13]telling them, "You are to say, 'His disciples came during the night and stole him away while we were asleep.' [14]If this report gets to the governor, we will satisfy him and keep you out of trouble." [15]So the soldiers took the money and did as they were instructed. And this story has been widely circulated among the Jews to this very day.

[16]Then the eleven disciples went to Galilee, to the mountain where Jesus had told them to go. [17]When they saw him, they worshiped him; but some doubted. [18]Then Jesus came to them and said, "All authority in heaven and on earth has been given to me. [19]Therefore go and make disciples of all nations, baptizing them in the name of the Father and of the Son and of the Holy Spirit, [20]and teaching them to obey everything I have commanded you. And surely I am with you always, to the very end of the age."

SESSION 3 EXERCISE

"God, I want to bring attention to you instead of me. I want to surrender my arrogance to you so that you are lifted up instead of me. I want to decrease so that you may increase. In order for this to happen, I need to make some changes in my life. Please help me with…"

SESSION 4 EXERCISE

"God, I want to thank you for…"

loving me even though I am a sinner.
For just being there even though I am
lost and tend to stray from your path
+ plan. You're always pulling me back
in. You have given me more love than
imaginable + Lord I AM NOT WORTHY
yet you bless me with your mercy, love,
kindness, and grace. You have
forgiven me even when forgiving
myself is not yet done. You sent your
one and only son for my unworthy
body + through him have washed
away my sin. How can I do anythi
besides lift your name + sing of your pra
You move me with your glory Dad + you
show me unending love Lord. You
have a purpose for me + meaning.
You give me purpose + meaning
DAD! Thank You. You make me some
without you nothing is worth it…

Feb. 21, 09   I Love You

WHO IS JESUS?

Jesus is God

The high priest said to him, "I charge you under oath by the living God: Tell us if you are the Christ, the Son of God." "Yes, it is as you say," Jesus replied. (Matthew 26:63-64)

Jesus became a person

The Word [Jesus] became flesh and made his dwelling among us. (John 1:14)

Jesus taught with authority

They were amazed at his teaching, for he taught as one who had real authority—quite unlike the teachers of religious law. (Mark 1:22)

Jesus healed the sick

Jesus went throughout Galilee, teaching in their synagogues, preaching the good news of the kingdom, and healing every disease and sickness among the people. (Matthew 4:23)

Jesus befriended outcasts

That night Matthew invited Jesus and his disciples to be his dinner guests, along with his fellow tax collectors and many other notorious sinners. The Pharisees were indignant. "Why does your teacher eat with such scum?" they asked his disciples. (Matthew 9:10-11)

Jesus got angry with religious oppressors

How terrible it will be for you teachers of religious law and you Pharisees. Hypocrites! You are like whitewashed tombs—beautiful on the outside but filled on the inside with dead people's bones and all sorts of impurity. (Matthew 23:27)

Jesus was persecuted

The chief priests and the whole Sanhedrin were looking for false evidence against Jesus so that they could put him to death. But they did not find any, though many false witnesses came forward. Finally two came forward. (Matthew 26:59-60)

Jesus was tempted in every way

... for he [Jesus] faced all of the same temptations we do... (Hebrews 4:15)

Jesus never sinned

... he [Jesus] did not sin. (Hebrews 4:15)

But you know that he [Jesus] appeared so that he might take away our sins. And in him is no sin. (1 John 3:5)

Jesus died, rose from the dead, and continues to live to this day

But Christ has indeed been raised from the dead... (1 Corinthians 15:20)

Jesus made it possible to have a relationship with God

For God so loved the world that he gave his one and only Son, that whoever believes in him shall not perish but have eternal life. For God did not send his Son into the world to condemn the world, but to save the world through him. (John 3:16-17)

Jesus can sympathize with our struggles

This High Priest of ours understands our weaknesses... (Hebrews 4:15)

Jesus loves us

May you experience the love of Christ, though it is so great you will never fully understand it. (Ephesians 3:19)

Sound good? Looking for more?

Getting to know Jesus is the best thing you can do with your life. He WON'T let you down. He knows everything about you and LOVES you more than you can imagine!

A SUMMARY OF THE LIFE OF JESUS

The Incarnation

Fully divine and fully human, God sent his son, Jesus, to the earth to bring salvation into the world for everyone who believes. *Read John 1:4.*

John the Baptist

A relative to Jesus, John was sent "to make ready a people prepared for the Lord." He called Israel to repentance and baptized people in the Jordan River. *Read Luke 3:3.*

The baptism and temptation of Jesus

After John baptized him, Jesus went into the desert for 40 days in preparation for his ministry. He faced Satan and resisted the temptation he offered by quoting Scripture. *Read Matthew 4:4.*

Jesus begins his ministry

The world's most influential person taught with authority, healed with compassion, and inspired with miracles. *Read Luke 4:15.*

Jesus' model of discipleship

Jesus called everyone to follow him—without reservation—and to love God and others. *Read Luke 9:23, 57-62.*

The opposition

The religious "upper class" opposed Jesus, seeking to discredit him in the eyes of the people. Jesus criticized their hypocrisy and love of recognition. *Read Matthew 23:25.*

The great "I Am"

Jesus claimed to be the bread of life; the light of the world; the good shepherd; and the way, the truth, and the life. Each of these titles reveals essential truth about who he is. *Read John 14:6.*

The great physician

His words brought conviction and comfort; his actions shouted to the world his true nature. Healing the sick, Jesus demonstrated his power and authority by helping people where they needed it most so they might accept the truth. *Read Matthew 14:14.*

The great forgiver

Humanity's deepest need is forgiveness and freedom from the guilt of the past—which separates us from God. Only God has the power to forgive, and Jesus further demonstrated his divinity by forgiving the guilty. *Read Matthew 9:6.*

The disciples

Jesus chose 12 ordinary men to change the world. They weren't rich, powerful, or influential. They had shady pasts, often made huge mistakes, and were filled with doubts. In spite of these things, Jesus used them to build his church. *Read Mark 3:14.*

The final night

On the night before his death, Jesus spent the time preparing his disciples, and he spent time alone. Obedient to the Father, Jesus was committed to go to the cross to pay the penalty for our sins. *Read Mark 14:32 ff.*

The Crucifixion

Jesus died a real death on the cross for the sins of the world. His ultimate sacrifice is something all believers should remember often. *Read John 19:30.*

The Resurrection

After dying on the cross, Jesus was raised from the dead by God's power. This miracle has never been disproved and validates everything Jesus taught. *Read 1 Corinthians 15:55.*

Want a more detailed chronology of Jesus' life and ministry on earth? Check out these two Web sites:

http://www.bookofjesus.com/bojchron.htm and

http://mb-soft.com/believe/txh/gospgosp.htm

SMALL GROUP ROSTER

NAME	E-MAIL	PHONE	ADDRESS / CITY / ZIP CODE	SCHOOL/GRADE

HOW TO KEEP YOUR GROUP FROM BECOMING A CLIQUE

We all want to belong—God created us to be connected in community with one another. But the same drive that creates healthy community can also create negative community, often called a clique. A clique isn't just a group of friends—it's a group of friends uninterested in anyone outside their group. Cliques result in pain for those who are excluded.

If you read the second paragraph of the introduction (page 8), you see the words *spiritual community* used to describe your small group. If your small group becomes a clique, it's an unspiritual community. You have a clique when the biblical purpose of fellowship turns inward. That's ugly. It's the opposite of what God intended the body of Christ to be. Here's why:

- Cliques make your youth ministry look bad.

- Cliques make your small group appear immature.

- Cliques hurt the feelings of excluded people.

- Cliques contradict the value God places on each person.

- Few things are as unappealing as a youth ministry filled with cliques.

Many leaders avoid using their small groups as a way toward spiritual growth because they fear their groups will become cliques. But when they're healthy, small groups can improve your youth ministry's well-being, friendliness, and depth. The apostle Paul reminds us, "Be wise in the way you act toward outsiders; make the most of every opportunity" (Colossians 4:5).

Here are some ideas for being wise and preventing your small group from turning into a clique:

Be Aware

Learn to recognize when outsiders are uncomfortable with your group. It's easy to forget when you're an insider how bad it feels to be an outsider.

Reach Out

Once you're aware of someone feeling left out, make efforts to be friendly. Smile, shake hands, say hello, ask him or her to sit with you or your group, and ask simple yet personal questions. An outsider may come across as defensive, so be as accepting as possible.

Launch New Small Groups

Any small group with the attitude of "us four and no more" has become a clique. A time will come when your small group should launch into multiple small groups if it gets too big—because the bigger a small group gets, the less healthy it becomes. If your small group understands this, you can foster a culture of growth and fellowship.

For Students Only

Small group members expect adult leaders to confront them for acting like a clique. But instead of waiting for an adult to make the move, shock everyone by stepping up and challenging what you know is destructive. Take a risk. Be a spokesperson for your youth ministry and your student peers by leading the way. Be part of a small group that isn't cliquey and don't be afraid to challenge those who are.

SPIRITUAL HEALTH ASSESSMENT

Evaluating your spiritual journey is important—that's why we've encouraged you to take a brief survey at the end of each session. The following few pages are simply longer versions of that short evaluation tool.

Your spiritual journey will take you to low spots as well as high places. Spiritual growth is not a smooth incline—a loopy roller coaster is more like it. When you regularly consider your life, you'll develop an awareness of God's Spirit working in you. Evaluate. Think. Learn. Grow.

The assessment in this section is a tool, not a test. The purpose of this tool is to help you evaluate where you are in your faith journey. No one is perfect, so don't worry about your score. It won't be published in your church bulletin. Be honest so you have an accurate idea of how you're doing.

When you finish, celebrate the areas where you're relatively healthy and think about how you can use your strengths to help others on their spiritual journeys. Then think of ways your group members can help one another to improve weak areas through support and example.

FELLOWSHIP: CONNECTING YOUR HEART TO OTHERS

1. I meet consistently with a small group of Christians.

1	2	3	4	5
POOR				OUTSTANDING

2. I'm connected to other Christians who hold me accountable.

1	2	3	4	5
POOR				OUTSTANDING

3. I can talk with my small group leader when I need help, advice, or support.

1	2	3	4	5
POOR				OUTSTANDING

4. My Christian friends are a significant source of strength and stability in my life.

1	2	3	4	5
POOR				OUTSTANDING

5. I regularly pray for others in my small group outside of our meetings.

1	2	3	4	5
POOR				OUTSTANDING

6. I have resolved all conflicts with other people—both Christians and non-Christians.

1	2	3	4	5
POOR				OUTSTANDING

7. I've done all I possibly can to be a good son or daughter and brother or sister.

1	2	3	4	5
POOR				OUTSTANDING

TOTAL:_____

Take time to answer the following questions to further evaluate your spiritual health. You can do this after your small group meets if you don't have time during the meeting. If you need help with this, schedule a time with your small group leader to talk about your spiritual health.

8. List the three most significant relationships you have right now. Why are these people important to you?

9. How would you describe the benefit from being in fellowship with other Christians?

10. Do you have an accountability partner? If so, what have you been doing to hold each other accountable? If not, how can you get one?

DISCIPLESHIP: GROWING TO BE LIKE JESUS

11. I have regular times of conversation with God.

1	2	3	4	5
POOR				OUTSTANDING

12. I'm closer to God this month than I was last month.

1	2	3	4	5
POOR				OUTSTANDING

13. I'm making better decisions this month compared to last month.

1	2	3	4	5
POOR				OUTSTANDING

14. I regularly attend church services and grow spiritually as a result.

1	2	3	4	5
POOR				OUTSTANDING

15. I consistently honor God with my finances through giving.

1	2	3	4	5
POOR				OUTSTANDING

16. I regularly study the Bible on my own.

1	2	3	4	5
POOR				OUTSTANDING

17. I regularly memorize Bible verses or passages.

1	2	3	4	5
POOR				OUTSTANDING

TOTAL:_____

Take time to answer the following questions to further evaluate your spiritual health. You can do this after your small group meets if you don't have time during the meeting. If you need help with this, schedule a time with your small group leader to talk about your spiritual health.

18. What books or chapters from the Bible have you read during the last month?

19. What has God been teaching you lately from Scripture?

20. What was the last verse you memorized? When did you memorize it? Describe the last time a memorized Bible verse helped you.

MINISTRY: SERVING OTHERS IN LOVE

21. I am currently serving in some ministry capacity.

1	2	3	4	5
POOR				OUTSTANDING

22. I'm effectively ministering where I'm serving.

1	2	3	4	5
POOR				OUTSTANDING

23. Generally I have a humble attitude when I serve others.

1	2	3	4	5
POOR				OUTSTANDING

24. I understand God has created me as a unique individual, and he has a special plan for my life.

1	2	3	4	5
POOR				OUTSTANDING

25. When I help others, I typically don't look for anything in return.

1	2	3	4	5
POOR				OUTSTANDING

26. My family and friends consider me generally unselfish.

1	2	3	4	5
POOR				OUTSTANDING

27. I'm usually sensitive to others' hurts and respond in a caring way.

1	2	3	4	5
POOR				OUTSTANDING

TOTAL:_____

Take time to answer the following questions to further evaluate your spiritual health. You can do this after your small group meets if you don't have time during the meeting. If you need help with this, schedule a time with your small group leader to talk about your spiritual health.

28. If you're currently serving in a ministry, why are you serving? If not, what's kept you from getting involved?

29. What spiritual lessons have you learned while serving?

30. What frustrations have you experienced as a result of serving?

EVANGELISM: SHARING YOUR STORY AND GOD'S STORY

31. I regularly pray for my non-Christian friends.

1	2	3	4	5
POOR				OUTSTANDING

32. I invite my non-Christian friends to church.

1	2	3	4	5
POOR				OUTSTANDING

33. I talk about my faith with others.

1	2	3	4	5
POOR				OUTSTANDING

34. I pray for opportunities to share what Jesus has done in my life.

1	2	3	4	5
POOR				OUTSTANDING

35. People know I'm a Christian because of what I do, not just because of what I say.

1	2	3	4	5
POOR				OUTSTANDING

36. I feel strong compassion for non-Christians.

1	2	3	4	5
POOR				OUTSTANDING

37. I have written my testimony and am ready to share it.

1	2	3	4	5
POOR				OUTSTANDING

TOTAL:_____

Take time to answer the following questions to further evaluate your spiritual health. You can do this after your small group meets if you don't have time during the meeting. If you need help with this, schedule a time with your small group leader to talk about your spiritual health.

38. Describe any significant spiritual conversations you've had with non-Christians during the last month.

39. Have non-Christians ever challenged your faith? If yes, describe how.

40. Describe some difficulties you've faced when sharing your faith.

41. What successes have you experienced recently in personal evangelism? (Success isn't limited to bringing people to salvation directly. Helping someone take a step closer at any point on his or her spiritual journey is success.)

WORSHIP: SURRENDERING YOUR LIFE TO HONOR GOD

42. I consistently participate in Sunday and midweek worship experiences at church.

1	2	3	4	5
POOR				OUTSTANDING

43. My heart breaks over the things that break God's heart.

1	2	3	4	5
POOR				OUTSTANDING

44. I regularly give thanks to God.

1	2	3	4	5
POOR				OUTSTANDING

45. I'm living a life that, overall, honors God.

1	2	3	4	5
POOR				OUTSTANDING

46. I have an attitude of wonder and awe toward God.

1	2	3	4	5
POOR				OUTSTANDING

47. I often use the free access I have into God's presence.

1	2	3	4	5
POOR				OUTSTANDING

TOTAL:_____

Take time to answer the following questions to further evaluate your spiritual health. You can do this after your small group meets if you don't have time during the meeting. If you need help with this, schedule a time with your small group leader to talk about your spiritual health.

48. Make a list of your top five priorities. You can get a good idea of your priorities by evaluating how you spend your time. Be realistic and honest. Are your priorities are in the right order? Do you need to get rid of some or add new priorities? (As a student you may have some limitations. This isn't ammo for dropping out of school or disobeying parents!)

49. List 10 things you're thankful for.

50. What influences, directs, guides, or controls you the most?

DAILY BIBLE READINGS

As you meet with your small group for Bible study, prayer, and encouragement, you'll grow spiritually. But no matter how wonderful your small group experience, you need to learn to grow spiritually on your own, too. God has given you an incredible tool to help—his love letter, the Bible. The Bible reveals God's love for you and gives directions for living life to the fullest.

To help you with this, we've included a fairly easy way to read through one of the Psalms. Instead of feeling like you need to sit down and read the entire book at once, we've broken down the reading into bite-size chunks. Check off the passages as you read them. Don't feel guilty if you miss a daily reading. Simply do your best to develop the habit of being in God's Word daily.

A 30-day Journey Through the Psalms

Imagine sitting at the feet of the pslamists: Old Testament poets and prophets who passionately cried out to God with the written word and offered visions of future events—even events in Christ's ministry. As you read through these emotional outpourings, try to feel and identify with the real-life circumstances of the authors.

Day 1	Psalm 1–5
Day 2	Psalm 6–10
Day 3	Psalm 11–15
Day 4	Psalm 16–20
Day 5	Psalm 21–25
Day 6	Psalm 26–30
Day 7	Psalm 31–35
Day 8	Psalm 36–40
Day 9	Psalm 41–45
Day 10	Psalm 46–50
Day 11	Psalm 51–55

HOW TO STUDY THE BIBLE ON YOUR OWN

The Bible is the foundation for all the books in the EXPERIENCING CHRIST TOGETHER series. Every lesson contains a Bible passage for your small group to study and apply. To maximize the impact of your small group experience, it's helpful if each participant spends time reading and studying the Bible during the week. When you read the Bible for yourself, you can have discussions based on what *you* know the Bible says instead of what another member has heard second- or third-hand about the Bible.

Growing Christians learn to study the Bible so they can grow spiritually on their own. Here are some principles about studying the Bible to help you give God's Word a central place in your life.

Choose a Time and Place

Since we are easily distracted, pick a time when you're at your best. If you're a morning person, then study the Bible in the morning. Find a place away from phones, computers, and TVs so you are less likely to be interrupted.

Begin with Prayer

Acknowledge God's presence with you. Thank him for his gifts, confess your sins, and ask for his guidance and understanding as you study his love letter to you.

Start with Excitement

We often take God's Word for granted and forget what an incredible gift we have. God wasn't forced to reach out to us, but he did. He's made it possible for us to know him, understand his directions, and be encouraged—all through his Word, the Bible. Remind yourself how amazing it is that God wants you to know him.

Read the Passage

After choosing a passage, read it several times. You might want to read it slowly, pausing after each sentence. If possible, read it out loud. (Remember that before the Bible was written on paper, it was spoken verbally from generation to generation.)

Keep a Journal

Respond to God's Word by writing down how you're challenged, truths to remember, thanksgiving and praise, sins to confess, commands to obey, or any other thoughts you have.

Dig Deep

When you read the Bible, look deeper than the plain meaning of the words. Here are a few ideas about what to look for:

- *Truth about God's character.* What do the verses reveal about God's character?

- *Truth about your life and our world.* You don't have to figure out life on your own. Life can be difficult, but when you know how the world works, you can make good decisions guided by wisdom from God.

- *Truth about the world's past.* The Bible reveals God's intervention in our mistakes and triumphs throughout history. The choices we read about—good and bad—serve as examples to challenge us to greater faith and obedience. (See Hebrews 11:1-12:1.)

- *Truth about our actions.* God will never leave you stranded. Although he allows us all to go through hard times, he is always with us. Our actions have consequences and rewards. Just like he does in Bible stories, God can use all of the consequences and rewards caused by our actions to help others.

As you read, ask these four questions to help you learn from the Bible:

- What do these verses teach me about who God is, how he acts, and how people respond?

- What does this passage teach about the nature of the world?

- What wisdom can I learn from what I read?

- How should I change my life because of what I learned from these verses?

Ask Questions

You may be tempted to skip over parts you don't understand, but don't give up too easily. Understanding the Bible can be hard work. If you come across a word you don't know, look it up in a regular dictionary or a Bible dictionary. If you come across a verse that seems to contradict another verse, see whether your Bible has any notes to explain it. Write down your questions and ask someone who has more knowledge about the Bible than you. Buy or borrow a study Bible or check the Internet. Try *www.gotquestions.org* or *www.carm.org* for answers to your questions.

Apply the Truth to Your Life

The Bible should make a difference in your life. It contains the help you need to live the life God intended. Knowledge of the Bible without personal obedience is worthless and causes hypocrisy and pride. Take time to consider the condition of your thinking, attitudes, and actions, and wonder about how God is working in you. Think about your life situation and how you can serve others better.

More Helpful Ideas

- Decide that the time you have set aside for Bible reading and study is nonnegotiable. Don't let other activities squeeze Bible study time out of your schedule.

- Avoid the extremes of being ritualistic (reading a chapter just to mark it off a list) and being lazy (giving up).

- Begin with realistic goals and boundaries for your study time. If five to seven minutes a day proves a challenge at the beginning, make it a goal to start smaller and increase your time slowly. Don't set yourself up to fail.

- Be open to the leading and teaching of God's Spirit.

- Love God like he's the best friend you'll ever have—which is the truth!

MEMORY VERSES

The word *memory* may cause some of you to groan. In school, you have to memorize dates, places, times, and outcomes. Now you have to memorize the Bible?

No, not the entire Bible! Start small with some key verses. Trust us, this is important. Here's why: Scripture memorization is a good habit for a growing Christian to develop because when God's Word is planted in your mind and heart, it has a way of influencing how you live. King David understood this: "I have hidden your word in my heart that I might not sin against you" (Psalm 119:11).

Challenge one another in your small group to memorize the six verses below—one for each time your small group meets. Hold each other accountable by asking about one another's progress. Write the verses on index cards and keep them handy so you can learn and review them when you have a free moment (standing in line, before class starts, sitting at a red light, when you've finished a test and others are still working, waiting for your dad to get out of the bathroom—you get the picture). You'll be surprised at how many verses you can memorize as you work toward this goal and add verses to your list.

"YOU ARE MY HIDING PLACE; YOU WILL PROTECT ME FROM TROUBLE AND SURROUND ME WITH SONGS OF DELIVERANCE." (PSALM 32:7)

"O LORD, OPEN MY LIPS, AND MY MOUTH WILL DECLARE YOUR PRAISE." (PSALM 51:15)

"FIND REST, O MY SOUL, IN GOD ALONE; MY HOPE COMES FROM HIM. HE ALONE IS MY ROCK AND MY SALVATION; HE IS MY FORTRESS, I WILL NOT BE SHAKEN." (PSALM 62:5-6)

"IT IS NOT GOOD TO HAVE ZEAL WITHOUT KNOWLEDGE, NOR TO BE HASTY AND MISS THE WAY." (PROVERBS 19:2)

"THEREFORE, I URGE YOU, BROTHERS, IN VIEW OF GOD'S MERCY, TO OFFER YOUR BODIES AS LIVING SACRIFICES, HOLY AND PLEASING TO GOD—THIS IS YOUR SPIRITUAL ACT OF WORSHIP." (ROMANS 12:1)

"FOR GOD IS SPIRIT, SO THOSE WHO WORSHIP HIM MUST WORSHIP IN SPIRIT AND IN TRUTH." (JOHN 4:24 NLT)

JOURNALING: SNAPSHOTS OF YOUR HEART

In the simplest terms, journaling is reflection with pen in hand. A growing life needs time to reflect, so several times throughout this book you're asked to journal. In addition, you always have a journaling option at the end of each session. Through these writing opportunities, you're getting a taste of what it means to journal.

When you take time to write your thoughts in a journal, you'll experience many benefits. A journal is more than a diary—it's a series of snapshots of your heart. The goal of journaling is to slow down your life to capture some of the great, crazy, wonderful, chaotic, painful, encouraging, angering, confusing, joyful, and loving thoughts, feelings, and ideas in your life. Keeping a journal can become a powerful habit when you reflect on your life and how God is working in it.

Personal Insights

When confusion abounds in your life, disorderly thoughts and feelings often loom just out of range, slightly out of focus. Putting these thoughts and feelings on paper is like corralling and domesticating wild beasts. Once on paper, you can look at them, consider them, contemplate the reasons they were causing you pain, and learn from them.

Have you ever had trouble answering the question, "How do you feel?" Journaling compels you to become more specific with your generalized thoughts and feelings. This is not to suggest that a page full of words perfectly represents what's happening on the inside. That would be foolish. But journaling can move you closer to understanding more about yourself.

Reflection and Examination

With journaling, you can write about your feelings, your situations, how you responded to events. You can reflect and answer questions like these:

- Was that the right response?

- What were my other options?

- Did I lose control and act impulsively?

- If this happened again, should I do the same thing? Would I do the same thing?

- How can I be different as a result of this situation?

Spiritual Insights

One of the main goals of journaling is to gain new spiritual insights about God, yourself, and the world. When you take time to journal, you have the opportunity to pause and consider how God is working in your life and in the lives of those around you. Journaling helps you see the work he's accomplishing and remember it for the future.

What to Write About

There isn't one right way to journal, no set number of times per week, no rules for the length of each journal entry. Figure out what works best for you. Get started with these options:

Write a letter or prayer to God

Many Christians struggle with maintaining a consistent prayer life. Writing out your prayers can help strengthen it. Begin with this question: "What do I want to tell God right now?"

Write a letter or conversation to another person

Sometimes conversations with others can be difficult because we're not sure what we ought to say. Have you ever walked away from an interaction and 20 minutes later thought, *I should have said…?* Journaling conversations before they happen can help you think through the issues and approach your interactions with others in intentional ways. As a result, you can feel confident as you begin your conversations because you've taken time to consider the issues beforehand.

Process conflict and pain

You may find it helpful to write about your conflicts with others, especially those that take you by surprise. By journaling soon after conflict occurs, you can reflect and learn from it. You'll be better prepared for the next time you face a similar situation. Conflicts are generally difficult to navigate. Thinking through and writing about specific conflicts typically yields helpful personal insights.

When you're experiencing pain is also a good time to settle your thoughts and consider the nature of your feelings. The great thing about exploring your feelings is that you're only accountable to God. You don't have to worry about hurting anyone's feelings by what you write in your journal (if you keep it private).

Examine your motives

The Bible is clear regarding two heart truths. First, how you behave reflects who you are on the inside (Luke 6:45). Second, you can take the right action for the wrong reason (James 4:3).

The condition of your heart is vitally important. Molding your motives to God's desires is central to following Christ. The Pharisees did many of the right things, but for the wrong reasons. Reflect on the *real* reasons why you do what you do.

Anticipate your actions

Have you ever gone to bed thinking, *That was a mistake. I didn't intend that to happen!* Probably! No one is perfect. You can't predict all of the consequences of your actions. But reflecting on how your actions could affect others will guide you and help you relate better to others.

Reflect on God's work in your life

If you journal in the evening, you can answer this question: "What did God teach me today?"

If you journal in the morning, you can answer this question: "God, what were you trying to teach me yesterday that I missed?" When you reflect on yesterday's events, you may find a common theme that God may have been weaving into your life during the day—one you missed because you were busy. When you see God's hand in your life, even a day later, you know God loves you and is guiding you.

Record insights from Scripture

Journal about whatever you learn from the Bible. Rewrite a verse in your own words or figure out how a passage is structured. Try to uncover the key truths from the verses and see how the verses apply to your life. (Again, there is no right way to journal. The only wrong way is to not try it at all.)

JOURNAL PAGES

JOURNAL PAGES

JOURNAL PAGES

JOURNAL PAGES

JOURNAL PAGES

JOURNAL PAGES

PRAYING IN YOUR SMALL GROUP

As believers, we're called to support each other in prayer, and prayer should be a consistent part of a healthy small group.

One of prayer's purposes is aligning our hearts with God's. By doing this, we can more easily get in touch with what's at the center of God's heart. Prayer shouldn't be a how-well-did-I-do performance or a self-conscious, put-on-the-spot task to fear. Your small group may need time to get comfortable with praying out loud, too. That's okay.

When you do pray, silently or aloud, follow the practical, simple words of Jesus in Matthew 6:

Pray sincerely.

"And when you pray, do not be like the hypocrites, for they love to pray standing in the synagogues and on the street corners to be seen by men. I tell you the truth, they have received their reward in full." (Matthew 6:5)

In the Old Testament, God's people were disciplined prayer warriors. They developed specific prayers to use for every special occasion or need. They had prayers for light and darkness, prayers for fire and rain, prayers for good news and bad. They even had prayers for travel, holidays, holy days, and Sabbath days.

Every day the faithful would stop to pray at 9 a.m., noon, and 3 p.m.—a sort of religious coffee break. Their ritual was impressive, to say the least, but being legalistic had its downside. The proud, self-righteous types would strategically plan their schedules to be in the middle of a crowd when it was time for prayer so everyone could hear them as they prayed loudly. You can see the problem. What was intended to promote spiritual passion became a drama to impress others.

God wants our prayers addressed to him alone. That seems obvious enough, yet how many of us pray wanting to impress our listeners rather than wanting to truly communicate with God? This is the problem if you're prideful like the Pharisees about the excellent quality of your prayers. But it can also be a problem if you're new to prayer and are concerned that you don't know how to "pray right." Don't concern yourself with what others think; just talk to God as if you were sitting in a chair next to him.

Pray simply.

"And when you pray, do not keep on babbling like pagans, for they think they will be heard because of their many words. Do not be like them, for your Father knows what you need before you ask him." (Matthew 6:7-8)

God isn't looking to be dazzled with brilliantly crafted language. Nor is he impressed with lengthy monologues. It's freeing to know that he wants us to keep it simple.

Pray specifically.

"This, then, is how you should pray: 'Our Father in heaven, hallowed be your name, your kingdom come, your will be done on earth as it is in heaven. Give us today our daily bread. Forgive us our debts, as we also have forgiven our debtors. And lead us not into temptation, but deliver us from the evil one." (Matthew 6:9-13)

What the church has come to call "The Lord's Prayer" is a model of the kind of brief but specific prayers we may offer anytime, anywhere. Look at some of the specific items mentioned:

- Adoration: "hallowed be your name"

- Provision: "your kingdom come...your will be done...give us today our daily bread"

- Forgiveness: "forgive us our debts"

- Protection: "lead us not into temptation"

PRAYER REQUEST GUIDELINES

Because prayer time is so vital, group members need some basic guidelines for sharing, handling, and praying for prayer requests. Without a commitment from each person to honor these simple suggestions, prayer time can become dominated by one person, an opportunity to gossip, or a never-ending story time. (There are appropriate times to tell personal stories, but this may not be the best time.)

Here are a few suggestions for each group to consider:

Write down prayer requests.

Each small group member should write down every prayer request on the "Prayer Request" pages provided. When you commit to a small group, you're agreeing to be part of the spiritual community, and that includes praying for one another. By keeping track of prayer requests, you can see how God answers them. You'll be amazed at God's power and faithfulness.

As an alternative, one person can record the requests and e-mail them to the rest of the group. If your group chooses this option, safeguard confidentiality. Be sure personal information isn't compromised. Some people share e-mail accounts with parents or siblings. Develop a workable plan for this option.

Give everybody an opportunity to share.

As a group, consider the amount of time remaining and the number of people who still want to share. You won't be able to share every thought or detail about a situation.

Obviously if someone experiences a crisis, you may need to focus exclusively on that group member by giving him or her extended time and focused prayer. (However, true crises are infrequent.)

The leader can limit the time by making a comment such as one of the following:

- We have time for everyone to share one praise or request.

- Simply share what to pray for. We can talk in more detail later.

- We're only going to pray for requests about the people in our group. How can we pray for you specifically?

- We've run out of time to share prayer requests. Take a moment to write down your prayer request and give it to me [or identify another person]. You'll get them by e-mail tomorrow.

Just as people are free to share, they're free to not share.

The goal of a healthy small group should be to create an environment where participants feel comfortable sharing about their lives. Still, not everyone needs to share each week. Here's what I tell my small group:

As a small group we're here to support one another in prayer. This doesn't mean that everyone has to share something. In fact, don't assume you have to share at all. There's no need to make up prayer requests just to have something to say. If you have something you'd like the group to pray for, let us know. If not, that's fine, too.

No gossip allowed.

Don't allow sharing prayer requests to become an excuse for gossip. If you're not part of the problem or solution, consider the information gossip. Share the request without the story behind it—that helps prevent gossip. Also speak in general terms without giving names or details ("I have a friend who's in trouble. God knows who it is. Pray for me that I can be a good friend.").

If a prayer request starts going astray, someone should kindly intercede, perhaps with a question such as, "How can we pray for you in this situation?"

Don't give advice or try to fix the problem.

When people share their struggles and problems, a common response is to try to fix the problem by offering advice. At the right time, the group might provide input on a particular problem, but during prayer time, keep focused on praying for the need. Often God's best work in a person's life comes through times of struggle and pain.

Keep in touch.

Make sure you exchange phone numbers and e-mail addresses before you leave the first meeting. That way you can contact someone who needs prayer or encouragement before the next time your group meets. You can write each person's contact information on the "Small Group Roster" (page 101).

PRAYER OPTIONS

There's no single, correct way to end all your sessions. In addition to the options provided in each session, here are some additional ideas.

During the Small Group Gathering

- One person closes in prayer for the entire group.

- Pray silently. Have one person close the silent prayer time after a while with "amen."

- The leader or another group member prays out loud for each person in the group.

- Everyone prays for one request or person. This can be done randomly during prayer or, as the request is shared, a willing person can announce, "I'll pray for that."

- Everyone who wants to pray takes a turn. Not everyone needs to pray out loud.

- Split the group into half and pray together in smaller groups.

- Pair up and pray for each other.

- On occasion, each person can share what he or she is thankful for before a prayer request, so prayer requests don't become negative from focusing only on problems. Prayer isn't just asking for stuff—it also includes praising God and being thankful for his generosity toward us.

- If you're having an animated discussion about a Bible passage or a life situation, don't feel like you must cut it short for prayer requests. Use it as an opportunity to add a little variety to the prayer time by praying some other day between sessions.

Outside the Group Time

You can use these options if you run out of time to pray during the meeting or in addition to prayer during the meeting.

- Send prayer requests to each other via e-mail.

- Pick prayer partners and phone each other during the week.

- Have each person in the small group choose a day to pray for everyone in the group. Perhaps you can work it out to have each day of the week covered. Let participants report back at each meeting for accountability.

- Have each person pray for just one other person in the group for the entire week. (Everyone prays for the person on the left or on the right or draw names.)

PRAYER REQUEST LOG

DATE

NAME

REQUEST

ANSWER

PRAYER REQUEST LOG

DATE	NAME	REQUEST	ANSWER

PRAYER REQUEST LOG

DATE

NAME

REQUEST

ANSWER

PRAYER REQUEST LOG

DATE	NAME	REQUEST	ANSWER

PRAYER REQUEST LOG

DATE

NAME

REQUEST

ANSWER

PRAYER REQUEST LOG

DATE	NAME	REQUEST	ANSWER

EXPERIENCING CHRIST TOGETHER FOR A YEAR

Your group will benefit the most if you work through the entire EXPE-RIENCING CHRIST TOGETHER series. The longer your group is together, the better your chances of maturing spiritually and integrating the biblical purposes into your life. Here's a plan to complete the series in one year.

Begin with a planning meeting and review the books in the series. They are:

Book 1—Beginning in Jesus: Six Sessions on the Life of Christ

Book 2—Connecting in Jesus: Six Sessions on Fellowship

Book 3—Growing in Jesus: Six Sessions on Discipleship

Book 4—Serving Like Jesus: Six Sessions on Ministry

Book 5—Sharing Jesus: Six Sessions on Evangelism

Book 6—Surrendering to Jesus: Six Sessions on Worship

We recommend you begin with *Book 1—Beginning in Jesus: Six Sessions on the Life of Christ,* because it contains an introduction to six qualities of Jesus. After that, you can use the books in any order that works for your particular ministry.

As you look at your youth ministry calendar, you may want to tailor the order in which you study the books to complement events your youth group will experience. For example, if you plan to have an evangelism outreach, study *Book 5—Sharing Jesus: Six Sessions on Evangelism* first to build momentum. Or study *Book 4—Serving Like Jesus: Six Sessions on Ministry* in late winter to prepare for the spring break missions trip.

Use your imagination and celebrate the completion of each book. Have a worship service, an outreach party, a service project, a fun night out, a meet-the-family dinner, or whatever else you can dream up.

Number of Weeks	Meeting Topic
1	Planning meeting—a casual gathering to get acquainted, discuss expectations, and refine the covenant (page 18).
6	Beginning in Jesus: Six Sessions on the Life of Christ
1	Celebration
6	Connecting in Jesus: Six Sessions on Fellowship
1	Celebration
6	Growing in Jesus: Six Sessions on Discipleship
1	Celebration
6	Serving Like Jesus: Six Sessions on Ministry
1	Celebration
6	Sharing Jesus: Six Sessions on Evangelism
1	Celebration
6	Surrendering to Jesus: Six Sessions on Worship
1	Celebration
2	Christmas Break
1	Easter Break
6	Summer Break

ABOUT THE AUTHORS

A youth ministry veteran of 25 years, **Doug Fields** has authored or co-authored more than 40 books, including *Purpose-Driven® Youth Ministry* and *Your First Two Years in Youth Ministry*. With an M.Div. from Fuller Theological Seminary, Doug is a teaching pastor and pastor to students at Saddleback Church in Southern California and president of Simply Youth Ministry. He and his wife, Cathy, have three children.

Brett Eastman has served as the leader of small groups for both Willow Creek Community Church and Saddleback Church. Brett is now the founder and CEO of LIFETOGETHER, a ministry whose mission is to "transform lives through community." Brett earned his masters of divinity degree from Talbot School of Theology and lives in Southern California.